ANDY EC

RESTORED
& REVIVED

Weekly Word for Daily Living

SOTERIA TRUST

Published by SOTERIA TRUST

DEDICATION

I dedicate this book to Michael Mellows and Robin Kemp.
You make a significant difference to me and this ministry.

ACKNOWLEDGEMENTS

A special big thank you to every friend and supporter of Soteria Trust who enable us to share the Good News of Christ Jesus in Britain and other countries. Thank you also to all those who today provide sponsorship to children, young people, and workers in Nigeria.

Thank you, Michael Mellows, the chairman and a trustee of Soteria Trust. You are a faithful and dear friend. Thank you to Robin Kemp, trustee of Soteria Trust. Robin has been with me from the start. Thank you for your loyalty and affection. Thank you to Martin Kitcatt, a former trustee of Soteria Trust, for many years of assistance to build a school in Africa. I miss you. I am very blessed with very talented and great staff at our Emsworth office with Roy, Lekan and Jana.

Revd Everton McLeod has made a valuable contribution to this book. Everton has written chapters 43 to 46. He was an Anglican vicar for many years in churches in England. He accompanied me on a mission trip to Nigeria, where his preaching and ministry were appreciated by all. I am thankful for your time at Soteria Trust.

I would like to thank the beautiful children of God who supported and established the African mission school in Ibadan, Nigeria.

Thank you to: Revd Geoff and Jen Waggett, the friends at Christ Church in Ebbw Vale, Ian and Joanna, Peter and Wendy, Mike and Polly, Peter and Jennifer, Tim and Annette, Chris and Cathy, and the friends of Tom Dodd. I thank J.John and Killy for years of wonderful love and friendship.

FOREWORD

First, let me say something about my friend Andy Economides. Andy relates a little bit of our story in this book but way back in the 1970s – when digital meant something to do with your fingers, to have a 20-inch colour telly was to show off and when the Vietnam war was still raging and there was still hope of a Beatles reunion – we were students together. Indeed, we were more than fellow students: we were good friends. We both came out of the Greek culture which gave us shared tastes and distastes and a mutual sense of feeling, well, just not quite *properly* British.

Now when they are talking about friends, people often say of someone, 'I'm very grateful that he or she introduced me to . . .' But that phrase does not do credit to the gratitude I feel here because, quite simply, Andy introduced me to Christ and the rest of my life has been something of a long and fascinating sequel to that meeting. In fact, significantly, Andy did more than just introduce me to Christ; he encouraged me to go deeper with Christ and to seek the experience and power of the Holy Spirit. So, both as evangelist and spiritual mentor I owe a great debt to Andy. As you would expect we have stayed close ever since and I am hugely thankful to the Lord.

Now, secondly let me say three things about this book. The first thing is that it is typically Andy: wise, practical, and distilled from many decades of a faithful walk with Jesus.

The second thing is that these 52 weekly reflections are condensed. Each one of them could easily be enlarged into a chapter length study but Andy has wisely left that unravelling and expansion for you, the reader. He has sown seeds here for you to water and nurture into flourishing plants. Why not read one of these reflections weekly and consider it carefully and prayerfully?

The third thing is that these reflections are meant to surprise us. When I first read through the manuscript, I found myself wondering where Andy was taking me and what his overall theme was. Each week's topic was so different. Now, after thinking about this, I have decided that actually there is a lot to be said for this way of presenting things.

For one thing, the compilation of seemingly unlinked topics is there in the Bible: try the book of Proverbs for example. Equally, too, many great Christian devotional books have no overarching structure or theme. Think for example of Spurgeon's *Cheque-Book of the Bank of Faith* or Samuel Bagster's *Daily Light*. The fact is that surprise has its virtues. To be caught unawares by truth means that we must face it without any prepared defences or expectations. Surprise catches us off-guard, gets round defensive arguments and can go straight to the heart. Dare I suggest that under such circumstances we are more likely to hear what, through his Spirit, God has to say rather than what we would like him to say?

So here are 52 meditations by my dear friend Andy. A long time ago I listened to what he said, and I am very grateful that I did. May you have the same experience!

Grace and peace,

Revd Canon J.John
www.canonjjohn.com

ABOUT THE AUTHOR

A ndy Economides is an international speaker and author of eight books. He equips and inspires Christians in effective leadership, in reaching out and caring for the poor and needy. He is an enabler, helping and mentoring pastors and evangelists in their own tasks of ministry.

His work and passion are sharing the Good News of Jesus and bringing people to know and follow Christ. Particular emphasis is given to the maturity of (new) believers and in assisting people to reach their full potential.

Andy Economides is the founder of Soteria Business School (SBS) in Ibadan, Nigeria, West Africa. The school is affiliated to Chichester College, West Sussex, UK. Chichester College Diplomas have been awarded to successful SBS students on completion of the two-year Administration, Computing and Business course. Scholarships for young adults and children are provided through Soteria Trust with the help of sponsors.

Andy originally qualified as an engineer and worked for six years in research and development. For ten years he was on the staff of a church as the lay minister and evangelist. In 1989, St John's Theological College, Nottingham, awarded Andy the College Hood for Theological and Pastoral Studies. In 1994 Andy became founder and director of Soteria Trust, a registered charity. Andy ministers under the council of Soteria Trust. Revd Andy Economides OSL is an ordained Christian minister.

If you would like to know more about the ministry of Andy Economides through Soteria Trust, would like to receive the Soteria News, or would like to order any of the resources available, please complete the response slip at the back of this book or visit our website at www.soteriatrust.org.uk.

CONTENTS

INTRODUCTION

Restored & Revived provides a weekly word for daily living. May the Lord restore and revive you as you set aside quiet time to read, think, and pray. *Restored & Revived* looks at how the Holy Spirit can work in and through the life of a true believer. To help us do this, 29 messages are devoted to covering all 28 chapters from the early Christian church as chronicled in the book of Acts.

The difference between the western evangelicalism of Christianity today and the early church is like the difference between chalk and cheese. Restoration and revival in the power of the Holy Spirit is desperately needed. It starts with you and me.

Let us wait upon the Lord. Leonard Ravenhill (1907–1994) was an English Christian evangelist and author. He focused on prayer and revival. Ravenhill said:

A man who is intimate with God will never be intimidated by men.

I am especially delighted to have covered subjects that I believe will assist to restore and revive God's people, including: the baptism of the Holy Spirit, the second coming of Jesus, inspiring lives, boundaries, confrontation, abuse, and he hates or God hates (Malachi 2:16). Do we want God? Ravenhill said:

I'd rather have 10 people that want God than 10,000 people who want to play church.

May you know the presence and life-changing fellowship and power of the Holy Spirit and Jesus. Be renewed and refreshed and blessed by the risen Jesus. Shalom.

Reverend Andy Economides OSL

RESTORED & REVIVED

Restore to me the joy of your salvation and grant me a willing spirit, to sustain me.

Psalm 51:12

My First Car

My father Demetrakis (1933–1997) bought me my first car in 1976. The car was an old second-hand white Ford Escort Mark I. The car was originally manufactured in about 1970. It had a 1.1 litre engine, rear-wheel drive, and lovely black plastic seats. I used the car for work, to attend Hatfield Polytechnic (where I studied engineering), and for pleasure.

Today, at the back of my home is a specialist car restoration garage. The owners of this business are highly skilled restorers and mechanics who restore classic cars. The garage has restored a Ford Escort Mark I which was originally built 50 years ago in 1971. The restorers have replaced the engine with a new fantastic reconditioned 2 litre Cosworth engine. Every aspect of the car has been more than perfectly restored.

The creators and mechanics have brought the car back to its original state by rebuilding, repairing, and respraying. However, they have also upgraded the 50-year-old car. The stunning red glossy Ford Escort with a white strip now has a bigger and better engine. The red car is 'a thing of beauty and a joy forever' (John Keats, poet, 1795–1821). Cars like this sell today for over £32,000.

Restored and Revived

To restore means to bring back to the original state. It means to bring dignity. To be revived means to come or bring back life or strength. The purpose of this book is to enable people to be restored and revived by His grace and Holy Spirit. And as in the case of the Ford Escort, to be more beautiful than ever before. The Lord says:

> *So I will restore to you the years that the swarming locust has eaten, the crawling locust, the consuming locust, and the chewing locust, My great army which I sent among you.*
>
> *Joel 2:25 (NKJV)*

Kintsugi, Japanese Gold Repair

Kintsugi is the Japanese art of putting broken pottery pieces together with a gold liquid. It is an art that is more than 400 years old. It not only restores and revives broken pottery, but the final article is more beautiful with its scars.

Treasure in Fragile Clay Jars

We who belong to and know Jesus have His light and life and His Holy Spirit living in our hearts. In our lives. His presence is within our fragile clay 'jars'. You have treasure within. Treasure in earthen vessels. Listen to what you have, to who you are, from Paul's word to the children of God in Corinth:

> *We now have this light shining in our hearts, but we ourselves are like fragile clay jars containing this great treasure. This makes it clear that our great power is from God, not from ourselves.*
>
> *2 Corinthians 4:7 (NLT)*

JESUS'S SECOND COMING

Then will appear the sign of the Son of Man in heaven. And then all the peoples of the earth will mourn when they see the Son of Man coming on the clouds of heaven, with power and great glory. And he will send his angels with a loud trumpet call, and they will gather his elect from the four winds, from one end of the heavens to the other.

Matthew 24:30-31

The Beginning of Sorrows

Our creator, our sovereign Lord is in control. Do not fear. The apostle Paul encourages us to set our minds on things above, not on earthly things. Eternity. The second coming of Jesus is coming. Jesus asks us, *'When I, the Son of Man, return, how many will I find who have faith?'* (Luke 18:8 NLT). Each of us needs to answer His question. Will Jesus find faith in me if He comes in my lifetime? Does Jesus find faith in me now?

Jesus Christ is the only Son of God and the greatest prophet. The prophet Jesus foretold of future events in the world. Jesus foretells of the destruction of the Jewish temple in Jerusalem (Matthew

21

24:1-2). This was fulfilled literally in AD70, when the Romans destroyed the temple buildings and Jerusalem.

Jesus Foretells the Future

Jesus is prophesying in detail of the signs of the end of the age: the coming of the Antichrist (or 'the man of lawlessness'), the Good News of the Kingdom preached throughout the whole world, and His own second coming or return (Matthew 24, Luke 21, also see 2 Thessalonians 2:3-4 and Revelation 13:11-18).

Jesus foretells about the beginning of the horrors to come or the beginning of birth pains (Matthew 24:8), namely:

1. False messiahs coming, leading many astray.
2. Wars.
3. Nations fighting nations, kingdoms fighting kingdoms.
4. Famines.
5. Earthquakes.
6. Pestilences (viruses, diseases).

All these represent the beginning of birth pains of the coming age. Jesus continues, saying about further birth pains in His discourse with His beloved disciples:

7. Worldwide persecution of Christians.
8. Apostasy and betrayal among Christians.
9. False prophets appearing and deceiving many.
10. Increase in wickedness.
11. Love growing cold.

End Times

Jesus says about end times, *'But he who endures to the end shall be saved. And this gospel of the kingdom will be preached in all the world as a witness to all the nations, and then the end will come' (Matthew 24:13-14 NKJV)*. Derek Prince in his book, Prophetic Guide to the End Times, says:

> We know that the nearer the birth of a baby, the more frequent and more intense the birth pains become until the baby is eventually born. In the same way Jesus says that once these birth pains start in human history, they will become more frequent and more intense. There is no way of reversing that process, the birth will occur.[1]

Eternal Life

For God so loved the world that He gave His only begotten Son, that whoever believes in Him should not perish but have everlasting life.
John 3:16 (NKJV)

Destination

People are going to one or two destinations: heaven (eternal life) or hell. Without Jesus the Saviour, people perish after they die. And without knowing it humanity is perishing in their earthly life, without Jesus. How can they live without Jesus? But whoever believes in the cross of Jesus, God's Son, has eternal life. Jesus offers life in all its fulness in this life, even though we may have suffering, hardship, or sickness. Believe and receive Jesus.

Turn, Trust, Take

Turn from your way, your sin, to follow Jesus. *Trust* in Jesus's cross to cleanse you from your sin. *Take* Jesus's precious gift of His Holy Spirit. A decision to surrender.

Decision Prayer to Surrender

Lord Jesus Christ, I know I have sinned in my thoughts, words, and actions. There are so many good things I have not done. There are so many bad things I have done. I am sorry for my sins and turn from everything I know to be wrong. You gave Your life on the cross for me. I put my trust in Your cross. Gratefully, I give my life to You. I ask You to come into my life. Lord Jesus, I receive (take) Your Holy Spirit. Come in as my Saviour to cleanse me. Come in as my Lord to control me. Come in as my friend to be with me. And I will serve You all the remaining years of my life in complete obedience. Amen.

THE PROMISE OF THE FATHER

Do not leave Jerusalem until the Father sends you the gift he promised, as I told you before. John baptised with water, but in just a few days you will be baptised with the Holy Spirit.

Acts 1:4-5 (NLT)

The book The Acts of the Apostles in the Holy Bible is a continuation of the gospel according to Luke, the historian, physician, and serious disciple of Jesus Christ. Acts should be called 'Acts of the Holy Spirit' through the apostles. The most important feature of Acts is the activity of the Holy Spirit, the third person of the Trinity. He, the Holy Spirit, comes with power upon the believers, including the apostles in Jerusalem on the day of Pentecost. The 120 disciples receive the baptism of the Holy Spirit, an outpouring of power. Have you received this Spirit baptism?

The Holy Spirit continued to empower, guide, and strengthen the believers and the apostles. Signs, wonders, healings, conversions, and powerful Holy Spirit preaching occurs. As a consequence, thousands of people accept Jesus as the Son of God and Messiah.

It is God at work through human channels. The Holy Spirit baptises with fire. It is revival.

Baptism of the Holy Spirit

These 120 disciples belonged to the Lord Jesus before the day of Pentecost. They were reconciled to God, born again, thereby converted and saved before Pentecost. It is by faith that they were saved (secured eternal life) and that was not of their own good works or merit. It was a gift of God (Ephesians 2:8).

It is unscriptural to suggest these 120 followers of Jesus were born again on the day of Pentecost. Some have wrongly suggested that these disciples had a born-again experience at the same time as their baptism with the Holy Spirit. Revd Anthony Chamberlain, in his excellent book *The Promise of the Father,* writes:

> *Jesus told His disciples that the Holy Spirit was already with them. However, the Spirit had not yet been given the medium into whom Christ Himself would baptise believers. The disciples on the day of Pentecost were the first Christians to be baptised in the Holy Spirit, therefore they set the pattern for us all: firstly, born again, then secondly, baptised with the Spirit.[2]*

Dr Martin Lloyd-Jones, a minister at Westminster Chapel, London, stressed that the sealing of the Holy Spirit, which he used interchangeably with the baptism of the Spirit, is a conscious experience and most importantly that it follows conversion. Dr R.T. Kendall succeeded Lloyd-Jones at Westminster Chapel, serving 25 years. In his book on the Holy Spirit called *Holy Fire*, he writes:

> *Dr Lloyd-Jones regarded the 'sealing' or 'baptism of the Holy Spirit' as being the 'highest form of assurance.' It was a conscious experience and something that follows saving faith.[3]*

RECEIVE POWER

But you will receive power when the Holy Spirit comes upon you. And you will be my witnesses, telling people about me everywhere – in Jerusalem, throughout Judea, in Samaria, and to the ends of the earth.

Acts 1:8 (NLT)

Joy

Notice carefully that Jesus strongly commanded His disciples to wait for the promise of the Father. Jesus said, *'Wait before you go, wait.'* Jesus told His beloved disciples that once they received the outpouring of the Holy Spirit, then they shall have power to be His witnesses. *'You shall be witnesses to me.'* The focus would be upon Jesus.

In the Summer of 1973, having left school, Kevin and I attended a summer Christian camp. I tell you the truth, I was not interested at all in Christian things. But it was an opportunity for sport, a holiday, and to meet other young teenagers. After about four days, one evening at 10pm, I decided to give my life to Jesus. I opened the door to Christ and asked Him to come into my life by His Holy Spirit. He did. Immediately on my return home, Kevin, his brother Neil, and I joined a fantastic youth fellowship. Although I was born again of the Holy Spirit, I was not baptised in the Holy Spirit.

Next Step

In 1974 at our youth camp holiday, I began to pray for more of God and particularly for His Holy Spirit. I waited in prayer for days. My youth leaders prayed for me. Suddenly, one late evening at the boys' dormitory, as I was praying, the Holy Spirit began to flood my being and heart. I was full of His joy and the Spirit's presence. I could not sleep because of the joy. I prayed, 'Lord, take some of the joy away so I can sleep!' Something happened. I was not the same. I found during the following weeks, months, and years, an ability to share Jesus with strangers or friends, anywhere and anytime. Many became believers and many still love and follow Jesus today.

The baptism with the Holy Spirit and fire makes all the difference to you and others you will meet. The promise of the Father to you is the baptism of the Spirit. Jesus says:

> *If you then, being evil, know how to give good gifts to your children, how much more will your heavenly Father give the Holy Spirit to those who ask.*
>
> Luke 11:13 (NKJV)

The condition to receive is simple: just ask with a sincere heart. Keep asking and waiting upon the Lord until He answers. The Father is more willing to fulfil His promise to you than you will ever know. Ask.

You need not wait for a special service. Remember to repent of any wrong ways. Confess any sin. Ask and believe. Find a place where you can pray, or ask a Christian friend to help you pray a prayer like this:

> *Lord Jesus, I thank You for dying on the cross for me. I give my life totally to You today. I ask You to forgive my sin . . . [mention particular things]. I renounce completely my involvement in . . . [let the Holy Spirit bring things to mind]. I ask you now to give me Your gift and baptise me with the Holy Spirit. I receive You now, Holy Spirit. Come, Holy Spirit. You are welcome. In the name of Jesus Christ. Amen.*

Spend a little time in quiet prayer, thanking God for His grace and goodness. Open your hands in a gesture of receiving. If you have asked and believed, God will keep His promise. We receive the baptism in the Holy Spirit once, for all time. However, we need to ask God to fill us with His Holy Spirit over and over again, every day, as we face certain situations and tasks. The 'formula' is simple: one baptism, many fillings, constant anointing.

The reason God anoints you is because He has other people in mind. This experience will not solve your problems, but it will add a new dimension of power and joy to your life which you never thought possible. May God bless you abundantly as you discover for yourself the beauty and grace of the Holy Spirit.

Prayer

> *The grace of the Lord Jesus.*
> *The love of God.*
> *And the fellowship of the Holy Spirit be with me.*
> *Amen.*

THE HOLY SPIRIT COMES

When the day of Pentecost came, they were all together in one place. Suddenly a sound like the blowing of a violent wind came from heaven and filled the whole house where they were sitting. All of them were filled with the Holy Spirit and began to speak in other tongues as the Spirit enabled them.

Acts 2:1-2, 4

Jesus instructed His disciples to wait to receive the power from on high (Acts 1:4-5, 8). The disciples could not carry out a supernatural task without a supernatural Saviour. All revivals in history need the preparation of the upper room. Jesus's disciples were gathered together, in one place, in one accord. They continued in prayer with 40 days of seeking. These are essential conditions.

When the day of Pentecost came, suddenly there was a sound from heaven like a roaring of a mighty windstorm in the skies above them and it filled the house where the 120 disciples were gathering. Then what looked like flames or tongues of fire appeared and settled on each of them. Not one person was left out, each was filled with the Holy Spirit. It was a baptism. They were immersed completely in the Holy Spirit. Then, they spoke in other languages or tongues as the Holy Spirit gave them ability. It was not quiet. It was messy and unusual and not religious.

Fire Falls

Revival is not about getting 'fired up' as much as it is getting under the 'fire fall'. In the natural, fire goes up. Elijah called down fire from heaven on the sacrifice. Fire came down on Mount Sinai. Fire came down on the day of Pentecost. Fire fell in Jerusalem because that is where Jesus told the believers to go.

Fire falls where God tells you to go. Fire falls on what Jesus tells you to do. Fire falls on obedience. Fire falls when you ask.

The Crowd's Response

The apostle Peter then stepped forward boldly proclaiming the Good News of Jesus saying, 'The Messiah, Jesus was crucified for sins, resurrected, and ascended to heaven.' Thousands were cut to the heart and said, *'Brothers, what shall we do?'* (Acts 2:37). You can tell when the Holy Spirit is working in the lives of people when they ask this question, 'What shall we do?' Peter answered:

> *Repent and be baptised, every one of you, in the name of Jesus Christ for the forgiveness of your sins. And you will receive the gift of the Holy Spirit.*

Acts 2:38

Three thousand people from the crowd accepted the message, were baptised, and added to the church. Several things may happen when a person is baptised in the Holy Spirit. Speaking in tongues, praising God, prophesying, or speaking the word of God boldly (Acts 2:1-4, Acts 10:44-48, Acts 19:4-7). The evidence of the Holy Spirt in a person's life can be the gifts of the Holy Spirit, power, love, and the fruit of the Spirit.

Prayer

Send the Fire
Thou Christ of burning, cleansing flame,
Send the fire, send the fire, send the fire!
Thy blood-bought gift today we claim,
Send the fire, send the fire, send the fire!
Look down and see this waiting host,
Give us the promised Holy Ghost;
We want another Pentecost,
Send the fire, send the fire, send the fire!
God of Elijah, hear our cry:
Send the fire, send the fire, send the fire!
To make us fit to live or die,
Send the fire, send the fire, send the fire!
To burn up every trace of sin,
To bring the light and glory in,
The revolution now begin,
Send the fire, send the fire, send the fire!
'Tis fire we want, for fire we plead,
Send the fire, send the fire, send the fire!
The fire will meet our every need,

Send the fire, send the fire, send the fire!
For strength to ever do the right,
For grace to conquer in the fight,
For pow'r to walk the world in white,
Send the fire, send the fire, send the fire!
To make our weak hearts strong and brave,
Send the fire, send the fire, send the fire!
To live a dying world to save,
Send the fire, send the fire, send the fire!
Oh, see us on Thy altar lay
Our lives, our all, this very day;
To crown the off'ring now we pray,
Send the fire, send the fire, send the fire!

This hymn about the Holy Spirit was written by William Booth (1829–1912). He was a British Methodist preacher who founded the Salvation Army.

TIMES OF REFRESHING

Then Peter said, 'Silver or gold I do not have, but what I do have I give you. In the name of Jesus Christ of Nazareth, walk.'

Acts 3:6

Peter and John having experienced the promise of the Father, the baptism of the Holy Spirit, are now changed men. Bold men. Better men. Key workers. Men able to love people such as the crippled beggar at the temple gate.

Peter and John passed the lame man many times before at the gate called Beautiful, but this time they are able, willing, and ready to be used by Jesus for healing. Peter challenged the man with faith-packed words and actions. Peter and John fixed their eyes on the lame man saying, *'In the name of Jesus Christ of Nazareth, rise up and walk' (NKJV). Peter took him by hand and the man started walking, jumping, and praising God (Acts 3:1-10).*

Revivalists

In those few moments, a revival of strength and health occurred all because a revivalist recognised an expectation to receive in a needy man's life. And then spoke the truth towards healing. True revival not only needs spiritually sensitive, faithful revivalists; it also requires needy persons capable of receiving those who can bring them life and are willing to obey their commands without hesitation.

Only because of this sign, people ran to see the healed man and the apostles. This creates Peter the opportunity to preach to them concerning Jesus's death and God raising Him from the dead.

> *You disowned the Holy and Righteous One and asked that a murderer be released to you.*
>
> *Acts 3:14*

Peter was calling the crowd to repent and turn to God so their sins can be wiped out. The revived Peter continued, promising them that if they did repent, times of refreshing would come upon them. Peter told the people to change their minds about Jesus, to accept the fact He is the Messiah, God's Son, and He died to forgive sins (1 Peter 3:18).

Change Your Mind

Repent means to change your ways. There are sins of commission: lying to my employer, employee or spouse, stealing from my work or government, not declaring properly what I earn to avoid tax, abusing people I love, not living for Jesus but doing life with little or no regard for Him. There are sins of omission: I could have been generous, I could have written or called but I was busy, I could have stopped but I walked by.

Please take this to heart. Peter's word is a promise for us, that times of refreshing will come from the Lord if we repent and turn to God. Be completely assured, God removes or blots out our transgressions (the breaking of God's law) and remembers them no more when we confess our sins because of the blood of Jesus on the cross. Believe. Turn to God and He will bring times of refreshing by pouring out the gifts of the Holy Spirit, the baptism with the Spirit. And after that, the continual filling and refreshing of the Spirit as you simply ask.

There is power in the name of Jesus. It was the apostle Peter's prayer in the name of Jesus that cured the crippled beggar. It was Jesus's name and the faith that comes through Him that brought healing (Acts 3:6). It is the faith and the baptism of the Holy Spirit of the apostles that brought revival. Two of the gifts of the Holy Spirit which He likes to give His beloved children are faith and healing. Let us eagerly desire these gifts for the good of others.

Prayer

Lord, I thank You for Your precious Son, Jesus.
I repent of my sin and turn my life over to You.
Forgive me. Receive me.
May times of refreshing come upon me.
May times of refreshing come through me.
Pour out Your Holy Spirit.
Lord, bring revival. Start with me.
I ask these things in the name of Jesus Christ.
Amen.

JESUS'S NAME FORBIDDEN

They brought in the two disciples and demanded, 'By what power, or in whose name, have you done this?' Then Peter, filled with the Holy Spirit, said to them, 'Rulers and elders of our people . . .'

Acts 4:7-8 (NLT)

Obey God or the Government

Intimacy with God, in revived lives, results in boldness of faith and actions. The believers, along with Peter and John, received a mighty baptism of the Holy Spirit and fire. The undeniable evidence of Jesus's impact on Peter and John and the healing of the lame beggar, and especially the subsequent preaching of a resurrected Jesus, challenged Israel's spiritual leaders.

Relationship with God increases ministerial capability and capacity. This was obvious to the educated men of Israel's Sanhedrin or religious council, but they were not pleased with Peter and John. The religious leaders – rulers, elders, and teachers of the law – brought Peter and John before men accusing and questioning, *'By what power, or in whose name, have you done this?'* Then Peter filed with the Holy Spirit said to them:

> *It is by the name of Jesus Christ of Nazareth . . .*
>
> *Acts 4:10*

The religious leaders, having heard the apostles' good defence, rejected it along with their Jesus. The council commanded them – yes, commanded the two apostles – not to speak or teach at all in the name of Jesus. But Peter and John replied:

> *Do you think God wants us to obey you rather than him? We cannot stop telling about the wonderful things we have seen and heard.*
>
> *Acts 4:19-20 (NLT)*

Religious Persecution

About 16 of us from the UK travelled to northern Greece to work together with the evangelical church and Pastor Costa in open-air evangelism in towns and villages. One warm evening, the team proclaimed the Good News of Jesus with a professional singer, mime artists and Costa and me preaching. We used a public-address system. Conversations between the team and the large crowd followed. However, a religious Greek Orthodox man complained to the police and reported us. Policemen came and removed Pastor Costa and took him to the station for questioning. We continued our conversations with the people gathered. Costa was released after some time and returned home.

The team and Costa had a choice whether to go again the second time to Eddesa. We went for the second evening. The same thing happened. The policemen arrived at the end of the evening and took Pastor Costa away for questioning. When the move of God occurs, persecution or difficulties are soon to follow.

We obey leaders whether they are Christian, political, religious or any other in authority until what is asked of us is against God or Jesus's instruction or word. We have not received the spirit of fear – or have we? Instead, we have received a spirit of power, love and self-discipline or sound-mind (2 Timothy 1:7).

The baptism of the Spirit and the continuation of being filled with the Holy Spirit makes the difference. Mighty are those who obey the promptings of the Holy Spirit. As soon as Peter and John are released, they found the other believers and told them what the leading priests and elders said. Then the believers were united and prayed for boldness.

Prayer for Boldness

Now, Lord, consider their threats and enable your servants to speak your word with great boldness. Stretch out your hand to heal and perform signs and wonders through the name of your holy servant Jesus.

Acts 4:29-30

LYING TO THE HOLY SPIRIT

Now a man named Ananias, together with his wife Sapphira, also sold a piece of property. With his wife's full knowledge he kept back part of the money for himself, but brought the rest and put it at the apostles' feet.

Acts 5:1-2

Fear the Lord

Ananias and Sapphira are bad examples of giving. The love for money and praise led to their death because they lied to Peter and, more importantly, to the Holy Spirit. This is a warning to us that, *'God cannot be mocked'* (Galatians 6:7). Ananias and Sapphira sold land and declared they had given all the proceeds to God's work. They had the right to keep back whatever they chose but made it appear they gave all. Peter confronts them about their deceit and lying. Peter says to Ananias:

Ananias, how is it that Satan has so filled your heart that you lied to the Holy Spirit and have kept for yourself some of the money you received for the land?

Acts 5:3

Ananias dropped down dead. About three hours later the same thing happened to his wife, Sapphira. Great fear gripped the whole church. Praise the Lord. Other people outside of church who heard about these events were also seized with fear.

Reverence or the fear of the Lord is the foundation of true wisdom (Psalm 111:10). We cannot act as if God does not see our lives. To have reverence for the Lord means to have regard in following His statutes, precepts, commands, and ordinances.

> *Fear of the LORD lengthens one's life, but the years of the wicked are cut short.*
>
> *Proverbs 10:27 (NLT)*

The apostles performed many miraculous signs and wonders among the people. More people were brought to the Lord because they believed in Jesus. People brought the sick out into the streets on mats and beds so that Peter's shadow might fall on them as he walked by and they would be healed. Crowds from villages around Jerusalem came to the apostles for healing (Acts 5:12-16).

Jealousy

The religious leaders instead of rejoicing that people were healed were filled with jealousy. With that jealousy within, they arrested the apostles and put them in the public jail.

> *Anger is cruel and fury overwhelming, but who can stand before jealousy?*
>
> *Proverbs 27:4*

Joseph, in the Old Testament of the Bible, could not stand against the jealousy that his brothers had for him. They almost killed him by throwing him in the pit. But Joseph was 'promoted' and vindicated.

David could not stand against the jealousy that was in King Saul's heart towards him. Saul loved David early on in their relationship but later did not. David had to remove himself and separate by running for his life because he could not stand Saul's attempts to kill him. Saul caused the separation. Jealousy is deadly. The Bible asks, *'Who can survive the destructiveness of jealousy?'* (see Proverbs 27:4).

Jealous Jezebel attempted to intimidate and kill prophet Elijah. Elijah was afraid and fled for his life. The Lord restored Elijah and dealt with Jezebel.

An angel released the apostles. However, the apostles were brought to the Sanhedrin who said to them, *'We gave you strict orders not to teach in this name'* (Acts 5:28). Peter and the other apostles replied, *'We must obey God rather than human beings'* (Acts 5:29).

These revivalists spoke up to these jealous, insecure, and religious leaders, pointing out that they killed Jesus by hanging Him on a cross. That they were witnesses to these things and so was the Holy Spirit, who God gives to those that obey Him. Bold, changed, Holy Spirit filled disciples.

The apostles were not killed but flogged and released. Revival costs. There is a price to pay for following Jesus and the Holy Spirit. The apostles left the Sanhedrin rejoicing because they had been counted worthy of suffering disgrace and flogging for the name of Jesus.

STEPHEN ACCUSED OF BLASPHEMY

And so, brothers, select seven men who are well respected and are full of the Spirit and wisdom. We will give them this responsibility.

Acts 6:3 (NLT)

It is recorded that the believers in the early church (Acts 6) were rapidly multiplying but there were rumblings and discontent. The Grecian Jewish disciples, who spoke Greek, complained against the Hebraic Jews, who spoke Hebrew, saying that their widows were being treated unfairly in the daily distribution of food.

The apostles addressed all the believers saying it would not be right for them to manage a food programme. Instead, the Greek–speaking disciples were asked to select seven good men to administer this programme. The apostles stipulated the qualification needed and that each man chosen was to be respected, full of the Holy Spirit, and full of wisdom.

The apostles made it clear and known to the gathered disciples that their own attention must be prayer and the ministry of the word. And that they shall turn the responsibility of 'waiting on tables' to the seven newly appointed men.

This idea pleased the whole group. They chose seven men and presented them to the apostles who prayed for them as they laid their hands on them. These deacons, or servants, included Stephen. Luke carefully writes other additional wonderful characteristics that Stephen had. Stephen was a man full of faith, full of God's grace, and full of power (Acts 5:5-8).

Full of the Holy Spirit, Wisdom, and Faith

Stephen performed amazing miracles and signs by the Holy Spirit among the people. These wonders and preaching pointed to Jesus. However, trouble was brewing for Stephen. That is what happens when the Lord is working, and revival happens.

Opposition arose from the members of the synagogue of the Freedmen. These were persons who had been freed from slavery who came from different Hellenistic areas. These religious Freedmen could not counter Stephen's wisdom, so resorted to lies and manipulation. The Freedmen lied that they'd heard Stephen speak blasphemy against Moses and God. Nothing good or godly comes from lies. Nothing.

You are a deceiver and fake if you lie in the name of God. You do not represent God or His ways by lying. Lying is wicked and sinful. Moses gave the ten commandments and said, 'You shall not give false testimony against your neighbour' (Exodus 20:16). God Himself does not lie and He tells us to be like Him and not to lie. Moses says in the fourth book of the Bible:

> *God is not a man, that he should lie, nor a son of man, that he should change his mind.*
>
> *Numbers 23:19*

The Freedmen hated Stephen and were prepared to remove him. The Freedmen produced false witnesses, who in turn testified against Stephen in front of the Sanhedrin. The revival work of the Holy Spirit through Stephen brought out what was in the heart of people. There is cleansing fire in revival.

Stephen was respected, full of the Holy Spirit, full of wisdom, full of faith, full of God's grace, and full of power. Stephen, a man of courage, with miracles, signs, and wonders, who preached Jesus.

RESISTING THE HOLY SPIRIT

But Stephen, full of the Holy Spirit, looked up to heaven and saw the glory of God, and Jesus standing at the right hand of God. 'Look,' he said, 'I see heaven open and the Son of Man standing at the right hand of God.' At this they covered their ears and, yelling at the top of their voices, they all rushed at him, dragged him out of the city and began to stone him. Meanwhile, the witnesses laid their coats at the feet of a young man named Saul. While they were stoning him, Stephen prayed, 'Lord Jesus, receive my spirit.'

Acts 7:55-59

The whole of Acts 7 is devoted to Stephen. It contains the most incredible sermon and courageous proclamation of Jesus before the religious council, delivered by Stephen. Within Stephen's address he focused on Moses who was a saviour for Israel. Moses brought them out of slavery in Egypt into their own promised land. Stephen spoke of Moses who prophesied the future saying, *'God will send you a prophet like me from your own people'* (Acts 7:37, Deuteronomy 18:15).

Courage

Stephen says to these leaders that they rejected Moses in many ways. The Jewish people did not believe, turned to idols, repeatedly disobeyed God's law, and complained against Moses himself. He says Israel also rejected Jesus of Nazareth, the Messiah. I can hardly believe the courage of Stephen who told them:

> *You stubborn people! You are heathen at heart and deaf to the truth. Must you forever resist the Holy Spirit? That is what your ancestors did, and so do you! Name one prophet your ancestors didn't persecute! They even killed the ones who predicted the coming of the Righteous One – the Messiah whom you betrayed and murdered.*
>
> *Acts 7:51-52 (NLT)*

'You always resist the Holy Spirit,' Stephen told the leaders. Stephen asks the leaders a rhetorical question on that day, *'Was there ever a prophet your fathers didn't persecute?'* No, is the answer.

Stephen Prayed to Jesus

Stephen stated that they persecuted and rejected Jesus the Righteous One. They murdered Him. The Jewish leaders were infuriated by Stephen's words. They shook their fists in rage. But Stephen, full of the Holy Spirit, not fearful, gazed firmly upward into heaven and saw God's glory, and there was Jesus standing at God's right hand.

That was it. They put their hands over their ears, shouting, and rushed at Stephen. They dragged him out of the city and began to stone him. The official witnesses took off their coats and laid them at the feet of a young man named Saul. As they stoned him,

Stephen prayed, *'Lord Jesus, receive my spirit.'* Falling to his knees, he prayed that the Lord would not charge them with this sin. With that, he died.

Stephen prayed directly to Jesus. Some people only pray to God in the name of Jesus. Some people do not believe you can pray to Jesus directly. But you can. Stephen did. I do. Praying to Jesus is possible and good because He is the Son of God, or God the Son. The Bible teaches the deity of Jesus Christ; therefore, He can receive our prayers and worship. Do not resist the Holy Spirit.

THE HOLY SPIRIT SPEAKS

As soon as they arrived, they prayed for these new believers to receive the Holy Spirit. The Holy Spirit had not yet come upon any of them.
Acts 8:15-16 (NLT)

Saul was one of the official witnesses at the killing of Stephen, giving his approval to his death. Stephen was buried. On that day, a great wave of persecution began against the church in Jerusalem. All the believers except the apostles fled into Judea to the south and Samaria to the north. Saul was going from house to house dragging men and women off to prison. However, the believers who fled Jerusalem went everywhere preaching the Good News about Jesus. Persecution spreads the gospel.

Philip went to the city of Samaria where crowds listened carefully to what he was saying about the Messiah because of the miracles and healings he did by the power of the Holy Spirit. People believed Philip's message about God's kingdom and the name of Jesus Christ. They were baptised but only in the name of Jesus. These believers had not received the Holy Spirit. Believers should be baptised in water in the name of the Father, Son, and Holy Spirit as Jesus instructs.

Key Worker: Philip the Evangelist

It seems Philip was perhaps unable to complete the task because he was incapable of ministering the baptism of the Holy Spirit to the people. Alternatively, was Philip unwilling to complete the task? In any case, the Jerusalem church and the apostles heard and observed Philip's ministry from a distance. Realising Philip was unable or, more likely, unwilling to do what was needed to minister the baptism of the Holy Spirit, Peter and John, both experienced in the laying on of hands for the required Spirit baptism, were sent to assist him.

The ministry of these perhaps more experienced leaders furthered Philip's evangelistic accomplishments. The fruit of revival can be extended by cooperation between ministries with mature discernment with spiritual actions.

As soon as Peter and John arrived at the Jerusalem church, they prayed for these new Christians with the laying on of hands to receive the Holy Spirit (Acts 8:17). The Holy Spirit was given, and this could be seen and felt by all.

The Conversion of the Ethiopian Official

Philip the evangelist is now directed by an angel to an Ethiopian eunuch, the treasurer of Ethiopia with great authority under the queen of Ethiopia. The Ethiopian was sitting in his carriage reading aloud from the book of the prophet Isaiah.

> *The Holy Spirit said to Philip, 'Go over and walk along beside the carriage.'*
>
> *Acts 8:29*

Philip ran over and heard the man reading, so he asked him what he was reading. The man begged Philip to come up into the carriage and sit with him. The Ethiopian asked Philip, 'Was Isaiah talking about himself or someone else?' Philip, using this scripture with others, explained it was about the Good News about Jesus.

The Ethiopian sees water nearby and instructs Philip to baptise him, so orders the carriage to stop. The Bible says Philip and the Ethiopian went down into the water and came up out of it and was baptised. When Philip came out of the water, the Holy Spirit of the Lord suddenly took him away, and the eunuch did not see him again. The eunuch went on his way rejoicing greatly. Philip, however, appeared at Azotus. He travelled about, preaching the gospel in all the towns until he reached Caesarea.

Ken

Recently I felt compelled by the Holy Spirit to stop and talk to a man I see in the street from time to time. I did not know him but this day I asked his name and we spoke. I invited Ken, who is 79 years old, for coffee and cake one day. A few weeks later we were sitting in an excellent café and out of the blue he asked me, 'Why have you invited me here?' I replied that I wanted to ask him a question and he was enthusiastic to know what that was. I asked Ken, 'When you die and you appear before God and He says to you (which He may), "Why should I let you into heaven," what would you say?'

Ken said to me that, because he has been good, he felt he would be accepted and have eternal life. I explained to Ken that our good deeds or good life do not and cannot earn our way to heaven or eternal life. All of us have sinned and our righteousness are as filthy rags. I shared that Jesus's blood and cross paid the penalty for our sins if we believe and trust. We are saved by grace alone, by faith alone, in Christ alone.

Ken listened well and asked me another question, 'What do you want me to do?' I told Ken to open the door to Jesus. Accept Christ as Saviour and Lord. Invite the Holy Spirit into his life (Revelation 3:20).

The Holy Spirit guides, speaks, empowers, heals, comforts, counsels, does miracles, lives in people, and is available. Ask Him.

JESUS INTERVENES

So the church throughout all Judea, Galilee, and Samaria had peace and was strengthened. Living in the fear of the Lord and encouraged by the Holy Spirit, it increased in numbers.

Acts 9:31 (CSB)

The church was spreading with more people becoming believers. At the same time, Saul was uttering threats with every breath. Saul had letters with permission and assistance to arrest men and women disciples and take them in chains to Jerusalem. The proud prosecutor who was going into Damascus as a conqueror to crush the disciples, was himself led into the city as a captive, to be forever afterwards the slave of Jesus Christ.

While upon his horse on his murderous mission, with his associates, Saul suddenly experiences a brilliant bright light upon him and falls to the ground, now blinded (Acts 9:1-9). A voice speaks to him, *'Saul! Saul! Why are you persecuting me?'* Saul enquires who is it that is speaking, and the voice replied:

*I am Jesus, the one you are persecuting! Now get up and go into
the city, and you will be told what you must do.*

Acts 9:5-6 (NLT)

Saul is now in Damascus. Ananias, a believer, has a vision with the
Lord telling him to go to Straight Street, to the house of Judas and
lay hands on Saul of Tarsus so he can see. The Lord tells Ananias
that Saul will take the gospel to the Gentiles, kings, and to the
people of Israel. Ananias would be responsible in leading Saul to
Jesus who in turn would turn multitudes to the Son of God and
Messiah.

Ananias the Revivalist

Ananias went and found Saul. When Ananias placed his hands on
Saul, the Lord Jesus gave him his sight back. Saul was then baptised
in water. God's errands are so important that we must not delay
in their performance. Ananias was told why he was to go. He was
told where to go and told what to do. It is the Lord's work. We,
likewise, should obey to carry out the Lord's work. Ananias was
reluctant to go, but obediently went. Had the revivalist, Ananias,
disobeyed God and resisted because of fear, we might not have the
largest portion of our New Testament writings in the Bible. That
is because Saul (Paul) wrote them.

Saul, the new disciple, spends days with the disciples at Damascus.
This initial fellowship is vital for Saul's growth. Within days of
becoming a believer myself, I joined other young people whom
I had never met before. They loved Jesus and welcomed me with
open arms.

Immediately, Saul preaches Jesus as the Son of God in the
synagogues. He confounded the Jews by proving Jesus is the

Christ. Some Jews plotted to kill Saul, but the disciples took him by night and let him down through a wall in a large basket. Again, the disciples looked after Saul. Saul had a new life and with it a new name: Paul.

When Paul arrived in Jerusalem, the disciples were afraid of him at first and would not believe he was a true disciple but someone who wanted to spy on them or harm them. However, Barnabas, an encourager, brought Paul to the apostles, telling them of his genuine conversion on the road to Damascus. Paul stayed with the apostles who accepted him. Paul felt welcomed and moved freely.

Then the church throughout Judea, Galilee, and Samaria enjoyed a time of peace. The church grew in strength and numbers. Notice that peace gives growth and also persecution. The believers were walking in the fear of the Lord and in the comfort of the Holy Spirit.

School of the Spirit Prayer

O dear Saviour, be not impatient with us – educate us for a higher life, and let that life begin here. May we be always in the school, always disciples, and when we are out in the world may we be trying to put to practice what we have learned at Jesus' feet, what He tells in the darkness may we proclaim in the light, and what He whispers in our ear in the closets may we sound forth upon the housetops. Amen.

Charles H. Spurgeon

WAITING BEFORE GOD

So I sent for you at once, and it was good of you to come. Now we are all here, waiting before God to hear the message the Lord has given you.

Acts 10:33 (NLT)

Cornelius With Revival Longing

Cornelius was a centurion who commanded a military unit of about 100 men. This Roman army officer was a devout man who feared the God of Israel. This captain gave generously to charity and regularly prayed. During prayer one day God spoke to Cornelius through an angel, giving him instructions to fetch the apostle Peter from Joppa to his home in Caesarea some 40 miles away. Cornelius sent three men to fetch Peter immediately (Acts 10:1-8). Revival began in Cornelius long before Peter arrives. It seems Cornelius already worshipped the true God, but this was not enough. He lacked faith in Christ.

Peter's Vision

The next day Peter is praying on the flat roof of a house in Joppa. He has a vision which includes a large sheet that contained all sorts of animals, reptiles, and birds. And a voice in the vision tells him, *'Get up, Peter; kill and eat them.' But Peter declared, 'Never, Lord . . . I have never in all my life eaten anything forbidden by our Jewish laws'* (Acts 10:13-14 NLT).

Three times Peter says, 'No, Lord'. Surely, when you say 'no' it ought not to be said to the Lord, and if you say 'Lord' you ought not to put side by side the word 'no'. Anyway, it is not for us to condemn Peter. Who are we that we should sit in judgement on another saint of God? We are not without faults ourselves.

Meanwhile, while Peter is puzzling over the meaning of the vision, he comes down from the roof to meet Cornelius's men. The next day, Peter and the others arrive at Caesarea. By this time Peter recognised that his vision had deep significance. Peter saw the barrier between Jews and Gentiles (non-Jews). The barrier has been removed (see Ephesians 2:11-22). Peter is, therefore, for the first time in his life, happy to come into a Gentile home and not to think of anyone as impure (Acts 10:28).

Peter confesses to Cornelius's household and staff that he now sees clearly (through the vision) that God does not show partiality. No favouritism. God does not show partiality among different people, cultures, nations, tribes (i.e. Yoruba, Igbo or Hausa), men or women, rich or poor, African or European. Cornelius had the most amazing attitude and expectancy when he said to Peter:

> *So I sent for you immediately, and it was good of you to come. Now we are all here in the presence of God to listen to everything the Lord has commanded you to tell us.*
>
> *Acts 10:33*

Revival attitude. Revival humility. Revival faith. Revival longing. Revival request. Revival day.

While Speaking, the Spirit Comes

The apostle Peter gives God's message. It was about God who anointed Jesus of Nazareth with the Holy Spirit and power. This Messiah healed the oppressed, did good, was crucified, God raised Him, and all who believe in Him will have their sins forgiven.

While Peter was still speaking, the Holy Spirit came down on all those who heard the message. There could be no doubt about it because the people spoke in tongues and praised God (Acts 10:34-46). Peter commanded them to be baptised straight away. Peter stayed with Cornelius's household for a few days. Revival.

There are several important lessons to learn from this revival event. One is the harvest of souls Peter reaped for the Kingdom would not have occurred had Peter maintained his traditional mentality. His traditional theology. His cultural bias. Peter changed his mind by God's grace and vision. To obey was 100 per cent necessary. When we change our minds to God's mind and our ways to God's way, we change our lives and the lives of others around us.

PROPHETS AND PROPHESY

During this time some prophets travelled from Jerusalem to Antioch. One of them named Agabus stood up in one of the meetings and predicted by the Spirit that a great famine was coming upon the entire Roman world.

Acts 11:27-28 (NLT)

Prophecy Needed

Agabus was one of the several prophets who came from Jerusalem to Antioch in Syria. Prophet Agabus received direct messages from God and communicated those to others. By the Holy Spirit, Agabus predicted that a great famine would spread over the entire Roman World. The Bible text also states that this famine happened during the reign of Claudius Caesar (AD41–54), the Emperor of Rome.

The prophecy given by Agabus was weighed up. It was believed to be a true word from the Lord. Therefore, the believers in Antioch began to gather money to send to the Christians living in Judea, and they sent that money by the hands of Barnabas and Paul.

You do not have to be a prophet to prophesy. However, a person must be baptised in the Holy Spirit to be used in any of the manifestations or gifts of the Holy Spirit (1 Corinthians 12:7-11). The apostle Paul says all can prophesy and gives helpful advice (1 Corinthians 14:31).

Prophecy: This is speaking the word of the Lord to others. It can be about the future and/or the word of God, spoken with power. There are different levels of prophecy and they can be delivered in a variety of creative ways. For prophecy to be fulfilled, certain conditions must be met. True prophecy has at least two basic conditions: faith to believe and obedience.

All prophecy should be tested because it is not always from the Lord and could cause damage. We often prophesy in part, which means that part of the word is not right. We must be careful not to throw everything out when there is some truth.

The person who prophesies should edify. Prophecy is to strengthen, encourage, instruct, and build up the church (1 Corinthians 14:4-5, 12, 26, 31). I have received several prophecies that have shown me how incredibly helpful and significant this gift is. In response, I have imparted prophecy to others to build up the church. It is perfectly correct to eagerly desire the spiritual gifts, especially the gift of prophecy (1 Corinthians 14:1, 12). All can prophesy (1 Corinthians 14:31). The church is weakened for the lack of prophecy. Do not show contempt for the gift of prophecy.

Preacher with the Gift of Prophecy

When a visiting speaker came to our church one Sunday evening, it turned out to be very special. The praise that evening was exuberant. Throughout the evening I was feeling expectant, that something would happen in my favour. I was praying that the preacher would prophesy the word of the Lord to me. I knew that this person had been used in this way before. It was almost as if I knew he would. I was full of hope.

When he finished speaking, he pointed to four individuals in turn and spoke an encouraging, comforting, and strengthening word to each. Gerald Coates spoke clearly, for all to hear. He then spoke to me, saying that in the future, doors would be open for me to speak internationally. He said I would be an evangelist to countries I have had no desire to visit.

Only 6 months after the prophecy was given to me, over 30 years ago, I travelled to Nigeria with three others to preach the gospel. We saw many people come to Christ. It was my first international mission trip. There would be many regular mission trips to Nigeria. And evangelism and training of leaders in Kenya (five times), Ethiopia, France, Finland, Denmark, Poland, Greece, and Cyprus.

Prayer

> *Oh Lord, open my eyes to see, ears to hear, and heart*
> *   to receive Your divine Holy Spirit.*
> *Oh Lord, pour out Your grace so I may receive all You have*
> *   for me for others' well-being.*
> *Lord Jesus, make me like You, who moved in the power*
> *   and gifts of the Holy Spirit.*
> *Lord Jesus, may I eagerly desire the gifts that strengthen and release.*
> *Holy Spirit, You are welcome to take over.*
> *Fill me again.*
> *Amen.*

KEEP KNOCKING

So Peter was kept in prison, but the church was earnestly praying to God for him.

Acts 12:5

Charles Finney (1792–1875)

There are always those who think true Christianity, or the move of the Lord and the Holy Spirit, is insanity. At Charles Finney's first public account of his own conversion, a fellow lawyer left the meeting with the comment, 'He is in earnest . . . but he is deranged.' When Finney stood up to preach his first revival message in the backwoods of New York, startling chaos ensued. One man came to the meeting with a pistol, with the intent of killing Finney that evening. Instead, he fell to the floor and was soundly converted to Christ.

Everywhere Charles Finney went for some 40 years, tumult spread. One preacher threatened to oppose him with cannon if he dared venture into his parish. Finney was denounced by clergy and society for his innovations in evangelism. Finney became the father of American and modern revivalism. He was unashamedly ahead of his time by the Holy Spirit. The world is never moved by the mildly interested. We have only two choices if we want to change the world: holy or unholy madness.

Some thought Finney was strange or mad. He was often rejected, as was John Wesley before him. Finney and Wesley had a holy madness. Charles Finney had an experience when the Holy Spirit came upon him and changed him forever. He was revived and, by God's grace, brought thousands upon thousands to a living faith in Jesus. Finney writes:

> *I received a mighty baptism of the Holy Spirit without any expectation of it, without ever having the thought in my mind that there was any such thing for me, without any recollection that I had ever heard the thing mentioned by any person in the world, the Holy Spirit descended upon me in a manner that seemed to go through my body and soul. No words can express the wonderful love that was shed abroad in my heart. I wept aloud with joy and love.* [4]

Holy Madness

We read (Acts 12) that the Lord and His Holy Spirit are working through His people and the apostles. As a result, there are wonders and people are being converted and becoming believers or Christians. However, there is further persecution and trouble. James is beheaded by Herod and Peter is imprisoned by him. The Lord miraculously releases Peter for the second time. There is little doubt that Herod would have killed Peter had he not escaped.

Peter arrives at the door of the gathered prayer meeting at Mary's house, the mother of John. The believers are earnestly praying for Peter's release. A girl named Rhoda hears Peter's voice at the door but does not let him in. Rhoda returns to the believers and explains Peter is at the door. The church cannot believe it. Even though they have been praying. The believing Christians are not believing. It is so funny. Anyway, they said to Rhoda, *'You're out of your mind'* (Acts 12:15).

Meanwhile Peter keeps knocking at the door. It was easier to get out of prison than to get into the believers' prayer meeting. Jesus gives us a promise, *'Ask and it will be given to you; seek and you will find; knock and the door will be opened'* (Matthew 7:7). Ask. Seek. Knock.

Prayer

> *My Father in heaven.*
> *Release me from my prison.*
> *Set me free.*
> *To know You, fully.*
> *To serve You, fully.*
> *To love You, fully.*
> *Lord, I ask, seek, and knock at the door of grace.*
> *Use me for Your kingdom.*
> *For Your purposes.*
> *For Your glory.*
> *Holy Spirit, You are welcome.*
> *Lord Jesus, thank You for Your precious love.*
> *Oh Lord, hear my earnest prayer.*
> *In Jesus's name.*
> *Amen.*

Jesus's Gifts to the Church

Now in the church that was at Antioch there were certain prophets and teachers . . .

Acts 13:1 (NKJV)

Revival Preaching in Cyprus

The prophets and teachers at the church at Antioch of Syria with other disciples were worshipping, fasting, and seeking God, when the Holy Spirit said, *'Set apart for me Barnabas and Saul for the work to which I have called them'* (Acts 13:1-2). When they finished fasting and praying, they placed their hands on them and sent them off. That is revival.

Luke says they were sent on their way by the Holy Spirit. John went with them as a helper. They sailed to the island of Cyprus arriving at Salamis. They began their first missionary journey.

Five Offices

In Ephesians (4:11) we are told of the five-fold ministry gifts of Christ to the church. That of apostles, prophets, evangelists,

77

pastors, and teachers, in the order of importance. In many parts of the world, the church recognises and has five offices.

In Nigeria, West Africa, where I have been visiting and ministering for 30 years, the church has all five callings. In Nigeria, there are about 18 million Anglicans alone. There are also different types of Pentecostal churches, streams, and denominations (i.e. Baptist, Methodist). These contain tens of millions of Christians. Many of these churches have the five offices as in the early church. These churches continue to grow fast. There is a need for prophets. There is a need for prophecy. This is lacking in the UK and Europe.

Sometimes we in the UK and the West think we know better. Sometimes we do, often we do not. Some Christians say 'those times' are over. My African friends reading this will say, 'No, it is not over until Jesus comes back.' Some teach and believe in God the Father, God the Son, and God the Holy Bible. In other words, we have the Bible now and we do not need the Holy Spirit to be active as in Acts or early church. This results in a weakened and powerless church. It is a pity.

Paul, in Paphos, is (again) filled with the Holy Spirit. He meets an evil man of the devil who is obstructing their preaching. Paul deals with the man, commanding him to be blinded. Immediately, the man became blind. That is revival. Sergius Paulus, the Roman proconsul, saw what happened and believed Paul's message. The sign confirmed the word. Again.

From Paphos, the missionaries sail 210 miles north-west of Perga and a further 110 miles inland to the city of Pisidian, Antioch. There on the Sabbath, Paul preaches to the Jews about Jesus the Messiah. Many reject Paul's message. Persecution arose against Paul and Barnabas. They announced to the Jewish people who rejected their message about Jesus, that from now on they would turn their attention to the Gentiles. The Gentiles did honour and accept Paul's message and were happy. That is revival.

After My Own Heart

Paul speaks of King David in his message to the people of Pisidian, Antioch. God said of David:

> *I have found David son of Jesse, a man after my own heart; he will do everything I want him to do.*

Acts 13:22

Think of it. The things the Lord wanted, David wanted. Their hearts and desires were similar. Therefore, David did all God wanted him to do. This is a statement God makes and it is true even though David sinned. Badly. He committed adultery and murdered the husband. His failure did not define David. God did not define David by that. David seriously repented. Restore unto me the joy of my salvation, David prayed (Psalm 51). That is revival.

Secondly, David served God's purpose in his own generation (Acts 13:36). That is marvellous. I feel I have served God's purpose in my own generation. I have served for 30 years in Nigeria, establishing four ministries that will, by God's grace, continue until Jesus comes. Come, Lord Jesus. I have served God's purposes by leading men and women to Christ who have become leaders and significant people of ministry and power today. Praise the Lord.

STAND UP STRAIGHT

This man heard Paul speaking. Paul, observing him intently and seeing that he had faith to be healed, said with a loud voice, 'Stand up straight on your feet!' And he leaped and walked.'

Acts 14:9-10 (NKJV)

Revival Signs Confirm the Word

Apostle Paul never did missionary work on his own. He always had at least another to share responsibility or to assist him. Paul and Barnabas arrive at Iconium having travelled about 100 miles from Pisidian, Antioch. Paul and Barnabas preach with such power in the synagogue that a great number of Jews and Gentiles become believers, that is disciples of Jesus (Acts 14:1, 21-22). The two stay there a long time preaching boldly.

The Lord proved or confirmed their message was true by giving them power to do miraculous signs and wonders. But there was opposition also, so Paul and Barnabas flee for their lives to Lystra and Derbe, continuing to preach the Good News.

In Lystra, Paul is preaching and a man, lame from birth, is listening. Paul, observing him intently, could discern that the lame man had faith to be healed. Paul said with a loud voice, 'Stand up,' and the lame man leaped and walked (Acts 14:8-10).

Faith Comes by Hearing

Faith came to the lame man through hearing the word Paul was preaching. Faith, a fundamental characteristic for genuine revival, is not achieved by preaching about experience. It comes through hearing with revelation in the word of God. Lasting revivals are built on the solid preaching of God's word. Revival preaching is what Paul and Barnabas were giving. Jesus will also be a focal point in the preaching.

Revival preaching requires revival and Holy Spirit preparation, ploughing the fallow ground of human hearts with the word of God for the moment. Faith comes by hearing and hearing the word of God. The message of God. Liberal words or teachings will not bring faith nor revival. Conservative evangelical teaching, which may deny the power and activity of the Holy Spirit today, will hinder saving faith. Get into the word of God, the Bible. Put yourself under biblical Holy Spirit teaching. Then revival can come to you.

Paul could discern that the Holy Spirit was upon the lame man as he was preaching. Notice Paul did not pray but commanded, 'Stand up.' Paul was flexible and always open for revival. Following the prompting of the Holy Spirit yet again, brought revival.

Trouble Ahead

The revival the lame man experienced brought persecution, as some Jews from Antioch wanted to kill Paul. They stoned Paul and dragged him outside the city, thinking he was dead.

But after the disciples had gathered around him, he got up and went back into the city. The next day he and Barnabas left for Derbe. They preached the gospel in that city and won a large number of disciples. Then they returned to Lystra, Iconium and Antioch, strengthening the disciples and encouraging them to remain true to the faith.

Acts 14:20-22

Eventually, they sailed back from Attalia to Antioch, Syria, where their journey had begun. Once they arrived, they gathered the church together and reported about their trip, sharing what God had done and how He opened the door for the gospel to the Gentiles, too. They stayed with the believers a long time. The first missionary journey of Paul and Barnabas was about two years long, in AD46–48 covering about 1,150 miles.

SALVATION

No! We believe it is through the grace of our Lord Jesus that we are saved, just as they are.

Acts 15:11

How Do You Go to Heaven?

Whether you and I go to heaven or hell when we die is directly connected to whether we embrace the gospel and Jesus. Our being saved or having eternal life cannot be separated from our welcoming and believing the gospel. Belief in this gospel can only happen by the Holy Spirit. Jesus welcomes all and does not turn aside anyone who comes to Him. Come.

Paul speaks of having eternal life (Romans 6:23) rather than going to heaven. He speaks of being justified by the blood of Jesus to escape the coming wrath of God (Romans 1:18, 5:9). Heaven not hell is what it comes to. Where are you going? Justifying faith is what saves us. It ensures us that we will go to heaven when we die. You are saved by putting your faith and your trust in the blood and cross of Jesus Christ. By receiving Christ. Your faith in the Lord Jesus atones for your sins. That is justifying faith.

To be justified means you are forgiven and made right with God, and you are righteous in God's sight. Justified means you are just as if you never sinned.

The Gift from God

Our works, no matter how many and wonderful they may be, will never, never, remove our sins. And our good deeds will never get us into heaven. Never. We are not saved by works. We are not saved by keeping the sacraments. Salvation by works is a human invention. We are saved by faith. It is a gift of God. A gift is free not earned.

> *God saved you by his grace when you believed. And you can't take credit for this; it is a gift from God. Salvation is not a reward for the good things we have done, so none of us can boast about it.*
>
> *Ephesians 2:8-9 (NLT)*

Perhaps the best way we know what we really believe (about going to heaven) is by asking: 'What do we trust when the time comes to die?' If you knew that you were going to die tomorrow, is it possible to be saved? Most importantly, can you know today for certainty and assurance that you will be with God in heaven? You can.

The apostle John wrote his letter and gives the reason for writing it: '*I write these things to you who believe in the name of the Son of God so that you may know that you have eternal life*' (1 John 5:13). Please understand and see the reason for his letter. John wanted the Christians to know for sure they had (past tense) eternal life. Saved. Heaven bound.

Some misguided Jewish believers in Jesus came to Antioch, Syria and were teaching. They insisted the Gentile believers could not become true Christians unless they kept the Law of Moses. And the text of such compliance was circumcision (Acts 15:1-5). Paul and Barnabas vigorously challenged this. The apostles and elders met to conclude what to do. Peter addressed the leadership saying it was not right to burden the Gentile believers with a yoke that even their own Jewish people could not bear. Peter says:

> No! We believe it is through the grace of our Lord Jesus that we are saved, just as they are.

> *Acts 15:11*

The matter was settled. A letter from the apostles and elders was sent to the Gentiles stating that it seemed good to the Holy Spirit and the leadership not to condemn them with keeping the Law of Moses and circumcision in order to be saved.

Be Saved

The gospel in a nutshell. Jesus's words: *'For God so loved the world that He gave His only begotten Son, that whoever believes in Him should not perish but have everlasting life'* (John 3:16 NKJV). People are going to one of two destinations: heaven (eternal life) or hell. Without Jesus the Saviour, people perish after they die. And without knowing it, humanity is perishing in their earthly life without Jesus. How can they live without Jesus? But whoever believes in the cross of Jesus, God's Son, has eternal life. Jesus offers life in all its fullness in this life, even though we may have suffering, hardship, or sickness. Believe and receive Jesus.

Turn, Trust, Take

Turn from your way, your sin, to follow Jesus. *Trust* in Jesus's cross to cleanse you from your sin. *Take* Jesus's gift of His Holy Spirit. A decision prayer of surrender.

> *Lord Jesus Christ, I know I have sinned in my thoughts, words, and actions. There are many good things I have not done. There are so many wrong things I have done. I am sorry for my sins and turn from everything I know to be wrong. You gave Your life on the cross for me. I put my trust in Your cross. Gratefully, I give my life to You. I ask You to come into my life. Lord Jesus, I receive (take) Your gift of Your Holy Spirit. Come in as my Saviour to cleanse me. Come in as my Lord and control me. Come in as my Friend to be with me. And I will serve You all the remaining years of my life in complete obedience. Amen.*

OPEN HEART

Lydia heard us . . . The Lord opened her heart to heed the things spoken by Paul. And when she and her household were baptised, she begged us . . .

Acts 16:14-15 (NKJV)

Evangelisation of Europe

The apostle Paul starts his second missionary journey in AD49 which lasts to AD53. This time Paul takes Silas with him. From Antioch they travelled through Syria and Cilicia, strengthening the churches firstly at Derbe, then Lystra. The Bible says the Holy Spirit told them not to go into the province of Asia and again the Spirit of Jesus would not let them go into the province of Bithynia (Acts 16:6-10).

That night Paul had a vision. In it, he saw a man from Macedonia in northern Greece, pleading with him, 'Come over to Macedonia and help us.' Paul and Silas decided to leave for Macedonia because they believed God was calling them to preach the Good News there.

Lydia's Conversion and Baptism

Paul and Silas boarded a ship from Troas landing at Neapolis, then inland to Philippi. Philippi was a major city in Macedonia and a Roman colony. On the Sabbath just outside the city, Paul and Silas went to the place people would usually go to pray. They spoke to the women gathered there.

Lydia, a God-fearing woman, a merchant of expensive purple cloth, was there listening carefully to what Paul was saying. Paul's teaching made sense and her heart was opened. She responded without a lot of commotion or manifestation. Lydia and her household were baptised immediately. Lydia wanted to know that she was acceptable to the Lord and Christ, and asked Paul and Silas to come and stay at her home if they felt that was the case. They went.

We do not need to be always looking for manifestations or heavy signs to indicate true experiences with God. Some people come slowly and surely to the place of conversion. We do not have to measure salvation on emotional response. What matters is only needing to be yielded to the Lord and allowing Him to do His will.

A Midnight Deliverance

There are times when such great signs do take place, as we see in the life of the Philippian jailer. Paul and Silas meet a young slave girl possessed with the spirit of divination. Her 'owners' make money out of her fortune-telling. The young girl is set free from this evil spirit by Paul and Silas (in Jesus's name and power). However, the owners have Paul and Silas imprisoned.

In prison at midnight, Paul and Silas are praying and singing hymns to God, the prisoners are listening and then a great earthquake occurs. Prison doors are shaken, doors opened, and chains loosened. The jailer is about to kill himself because the authority will kill him for allowing the prisoners to escape. Paul called in a loud voice, *'Do yourself no harm, for we are all here'* (Acts 16:28 NKJV).

The jailer is trembling before Paul and Silas saying, *'Sirs, what must I do to be saved?'* This is revival. Paul instructs the jailer to believe in the Lord Jesus and be saved – him and his household. Paul and Silas spoke the word of the Lord to him and to all in the jailer's house. The jailer and all his family were baptised immediately. The jailer rejoiced because he believed in God together with his household.

Some people experience Jesus loudly, others softly. Not everyone comes to Jesus and is saved the same way. Let us recognise that the Lord works quietly or loudly but be ready ourselves always to be blessed whichever way He chooses to come.

Prayer

Oh Lord, help me listen like Lydia.

Sometimes, Lord, You come quietly, sometimes loudly.

Come as You like, my Master.

Lord, help me be respectful like the jailer who said,

'Sirs, what must I do?'

Spirit of Jesus, I praise You.

Spirit of Jesus, speak to me.

Lord Jesus, hear my prayer.

Amen.

BABBLER. AIRHEAD. COCK-SPARROW

He went to the Synagogue to debate . . . and he spoke daily in the public square . . . they said, 'This babbler has picked up some strange ideas.'

Acts 17:17-18 (NLT)

Ministry in Thessalonica

By divine intervention, Paul and Silas are released from prison. They travelled 100 miles from Philippi to Thessalonica, passing through Amphipolis and Apollonia. All four places are in present-day northern Greece but then were Macedonian. Thessalonica was the capital. This city had a population of more than 200,000. Paul preached from the Scriptures in the synagogue that Jesus was the Messiah.

Some Jews, a large number of God-fearing Greeks, and some prominent women were persuaded, becoming believers. Years later, Paul writes two letters to the believers which are known to us as First and Second Thessalonians in the Bible. Again, there is trouble because of jealousy (Acts 17:5) and the new believers sent Paul and Silas away to safety in Berea which is 50 miles away.

The Bereans were more open-minded than the people in Thessalonica. They listened eagerly to Paul's message and searched the Scriptures each day to check up hat Paul was really teaching the truth. Many believed and received Christ, both Greeks and Jewish people. Some Jews in Thessalonica learned about the success of Paul's preaching in Berea and went there to stir up trouble. The believers stepped in, escorting Paul by sea to the coast of Athens.

Ministry in Athens

Paul is distressed to see the city of Athens full of idols. So, in the synagogue with Jews and the God-fearing Greeks every day, as well as in the marketplace, Paul is debating. A group of philosophers asked, 'What is this babbler trying to say?'

The Greek word for 'babbler' meant 'seed picker', a bird picking up seeds here and there. It also meant a loafer in the marketplace who picked up whatever scraps of learning he could find, and told them to others without understanding them himself. They called Paul an airhead. I like how J.B. Philips translates this verse in modern language, *'What is this cock-sparrow trying to say?'*

To some, the Christian message may seem nonsense or worthless. But it is talking about Jesus that matters. Talking about Jesus is the spark that brings revival. You and I are not responsible for the results of the message. We are responsible in getting the message out. Paul was responsible for 'babbling'. Some mocked.

It is like that in any revival. Revival is not all 'glory, glory, hallelujah'. There will be resistance or rejection at times. But under the sovereignty of God it is all 'glory, glory, hallelujah'. Some sneered at Paul's teaching of the resurrection of the dead, but others wanted to hear more. A few men became Christians along with a woman named Damaris. All this was worthwhile.

DO NOT BE SILENT

One night the Lord spoke to Paul in a vision: 'Do not be afraid; keep on speaking, do not be silent.'

Acts 18:9

Founding the Corinthian Church

Paul arrives in Corinth from Athens and meets a Jewish believer in Jesus Christ called Aquilla, a wonderful Christian it seems. Paul stayed with Aquilla and his wife Priscilla. Paul and Aquilla were tent makers and this supported them and their ministry. Paul was opposed by those who would not accept Jesus as the Christ (Acts 18:4-7). However, Crispus, the synagogue ruler and all his household believed in Jesus and many of the Corinthians who heard Paul also believed and were baptised.

People heard the Good News and responded, accepted Jesus, and were baptised. Hearing, believing, and being baptised (at once). This was the pattern in the early church. In many parts of the world this is done. In Nigeria, we baptise those who become Christians quickly. Almost every time I am in Nigeria, I baptise believers. If a young person becomes a Christian on Wednesday, they can be baptised on Friday.

The early church in Acts puts the rightful high value on baptism. Often, we do not do so today, especially in Europe. We need to learn from the African church. The church should instruct people who become Christians to be baptised. I became a true Christian, that is born again, in 1973 in my teens. But I was not baptised by full immersion as a believer until some 9 years later. I do not consider my being christened as a baby adequate. How can a baby hear, believe, and receive Christ? There is no evidence of babies being baptised in the New Testament of the Bible. The joy of being baptised as a believer is wonderful. Believers' baptism is meaningful and biblical.

Baptism. Communion. Oil.

In the Anglican church in England, there is the opportunity for those who were christened or 'baptised' as babies to be baptised as believers by full immersion. This is because the baptismal promises, taken as a baby, can be renewed. It has been wonderful assisting many people to be baptised by immersion in the Anglican church in this way.

Once upon a time I thought baptism was not important. Baptism is vital. These things are important: baptism, breaking of bread (holy communion), and anointing with oil for those who are sick (James 5:13-15). Where the Spirit of the Lord is, there is freedom.

Paul was again experiencing opposition and abuse in Corinth (Acts 18:6). You can tell revival is present when people oppose or insult. One night Jesus spoke to Paul in a vision:

Do not be afraid; keep on speaking, do not be silent. For I am with you, and no one is going to attack and harm you, because I have many people in this city.

Acts 18:9-10

Know this, the promise is as valuable as the fulfilment. Jesus told Paul, 'I am with you.' This cheered his tried spirit. To know Jesus was with him – approving, supporting, and defending him – was a safeguard against fear. 'I am with you' involves support. Jesus is working with us. He is on the same side, exerting His power in our hearts, minds, and lives.

Prayer

Lord, Your servant is listening, speak to me.

Lord, as Your child, I choose to believe You speak to me, through me.

Lord, Your word and heart is precious, thank You.

Lord, here I am, use me.

Jesus, here I am, send me.

Amen.

MIRACLES GLORIFY CHRIST

There he found some disciples and asked them, 'Did you receive the Holy Spirit when you believed?' They answered, 'No, we have not even heard that there is a Holy Spirit.'

Acts 19:1-2

Depending on Christ's Mighty Power

The Lord continues to lead Paul. Paul is working tirelessly with all the energy God gives him. He is empowered and motivated by the Holy Spirit. Paul is evangelising, making disciples, planting churches, pastoring, and training others to do ministry. There is much fruit. If the Holy Spirit had not been active through Paul, what results, or fruit, would there have been? What would have been accomplished? Nothing.

Paul is now in the seaport of Ephesus, modern Turkey today. There he found disciples of John the Baptist. Paul sees there is a problem and asks them if they received the Holy Spirit when they believed. They had not even heard that there is a Holy Spirit (Acts 19:1-7). Like Apollos, these disciples had a limited understanding of the gospel and did not have an adequate knowledge of Jesus. They lacked knowing about sins forgiven. More importantly, they completely lacked the Holy Spirit.

Paul swiftly baptises them in water. We learn what happens next.

> *When Paul placed his hands on them, the Holy Spirit came on them, and they spoke in tongues and prophesied.*
>
> *Acts 19:6*

Paul spoke boldly in the synagogue for three months about the Kingdom of God. Some became hardened to Paul's gospel message and Paul himself. They would not believe and were slandering the Christian faith. Those who slander the Christian faith and Christians suffer for it. God is watching.

Paul eventually withdrew himself from this abuse and unbelief. Paul took the true disciples away from this unacceptable behaviour. Instead, Paul held discussions every day with these genuine and dedicated disciples in the lecture hall of Tyrannus. Paul did this for two years. All people heard the word of the Lord.

Jesus's Name Held in High Esteem

God gave Paul the power to do unusual miracles. The sick were healed. Evil spirits came out of people. As a result, many became believers and confessed their sinful practices. A large number of new followers of Jesus who previously practised magic and evil brought their incantation books and burned them at a public bonfire. The value of the books was 50,000 pieces of silver. One silver coin was equivalent to a day's wage. In other words, the value of the books burned was several million pounds, and even more in dollars. This was serious repentance. They stopped practising evil which gave them an income. Their evil ways were a business. They could have sold the books, once they decided to stop the evil, but did not because they did not want others to continue in evil ways. They put their trust in Jesus to provide.

Stolen Books Return

A few weeks after I completed my secondary school education, I attended a Christian camp and became a Christian. When I left school, I had stolen some textbooks, but since becoming a Christian my conscience bothered me. The books were large and heavy. I remember returning to school carrying the heavy load. I quickly walked up to the second floor to see my previous form teacher, Mr Mallet, in my old classroom. I told him I had felt convicted so was returning the stolen books. I said I was sorry. He thanked me for being honest and let me go.

There is a cost to following Jesus. Revival costs in many ways. It can cost our reputation. Who cares? Jesus made Himself of no reputation. Revival can be humiliating and humbling. Revival means trusting Jesus and letting go. When we are aware of something that needs to be put right, we must act promptly.

Prayer

> *Lord, please do not allow me to limit what You want to do in me and through me.*
> *Lord, let faith arise and my doubts be gone.*
> *Lord, help me to trust You.*
> *To trust Your Holy Spirit.*
> *I trust You, Lord Jesus.*
> *Amen.*

FATHERS AND SONS

He travelled through that area, speaking many words of encouragement to the people, and finally arrived in Greece, where he stayed three months. Because some Jews had plotted against him just as he was about to sail for Syria, he decided to go back through Macedonia. He was accompanied by Sopater son of Pyrrhus from Berea, Aristarchus and Secundus from Thessalonica, Gaius from Derbe, Timothy also, and Tychicus and Trophimus from the province of Asia.

Acts 20:2-4

Band of Brothers

Paul escaped the riots against him in Ephesus and through the area of Macedonia encouraging believers. Paul then goes into Greece for three months ministry.

Several men were travelling with Paul: Sopater, Aristarchus, Secundus, Gaius, Timothy, Tychicus, and Trophimus. These brothers were helpers to Paul. They assisted Paul to fulfil the ministry, calling and preaching God had given him. They were also co-workers with Paul. These brothers loved Paul. They protected him and were faithful. Tychicus was a constant help to Paul

(2 Timothy 4:12, Titus 3:12). Paul especially loved Tychicus. Paul, writing to the Ephesians, says of him:

> *Tychicus, the dear brother and faithful servant in the Lord, will tell you everything, so that you also may know how I am and what I am doing. I am sending him to you for this very purpose, that you may know how we are, and that he may encourage you.*
>
> *Ephesians 6:21-22*

Again, Paul writing of Tychicus to the Christians at Colossae, says:

> *Tychicus will give you a full report about how I am getting along. He is a beloved brother and faithful helper who serves with me in the Lord's work.*
>
> *Colossians 4:7 (NLT)*

Timothy

Paul wrote two pastoral letters to Timothy. Timothy was Paul's 'fellow worker'. Of him Paul could say, *'I have no one else like him'* (Philippian 2:20). Writing to Timothy Paul says:

> *To Timothy my true son in the faith . . .*
>
> *1 Timothy 1:2*

Timothy was Paul's spiritual son. Paul would not have loved Timothy more if he was his actual blood son. Timothy owed his spiritual life to Paul. And spiritual life affects every area of physical life. Paul believed in Timothy as a pastor who also did the work of an evangelist.

The Lord Jesus called Paul to evangelise many countries and areas – the Middle East and much of Europe. To do that, Jesus supplied Paul men and women to fulfil that calling. In the process, men like Timothy found their calling and destiny. Timothy was wonderfully 'twined' and in union with a father figure, Paul. Timothy loved Paul with affection.

Paul and Timothy were two people with different backgrounds and ages, brought together for God's glory. And for the expansion of God's Kingdom. That is revival. A union like that has anointing. Unity with the Holy Spirit brings revival.

Reverend Canon J.John MA

During my student days in London, I studied engineering. In my first year at college I met J.John and over a period of six months became very good friends. Throughout, I was praying for his conversion. I introduced J.John to Jesus and he became a Christian in 1975. Immediately, that very week, I started to disciple him.

We met for fun, fellowship, Bible study, evangelism, and he attended our youth fellowship, which was fantastic. I was a Paul to J.John and he was like a Timothy, a son in the Lord. Today he is like a Paul to me. J.John is an international evangelist and author. Thousands have come to Christ through J.John's preaching, training, and work.

Evangelists, Associates, and Brothers

Today, J.John and I lead a band of brothers. Twelve men who journey together through the ups and downs of life, who assist one another in ministry and sometimes who work together on God's assignments. Twelve men who are true friends with true relationships. Twelve evangelists, each with significant and amazingly different ministries.

The brothers have an annual retreat over three days at a good hotel. At each retreat, every man has an opportunity to share about personal and ministry matters for about 20 minutes while the rest carefully listen. Then the person who shared gets seriously prayed for. Often words are given as the Holy Spirit leads. Advice is given. Correction is never held back. Encouragement is poured out. Love abounds.

A few years ago, a brother came to the retreat having already decided he was going to come out of full-time ministry. He did not tell us, but the Lord used the visiting prophetic guest speaker to speak over Gordon's life. Gordon (not his real name) had reached rock bottom. Like Joseph in the pit. At the start of the retreat, he was totally discouraged. Gordon was like Elijah who was anointed but distressed. Elijah ran for his life to get away from the troublesome evil woman, Jezebel. At one moment in the meeting, without warning, the speaker addressed Gordon in front of us all. He knew in his spirit about Gordon's situation and the (wrong) decision to give up. The speaker prophesied over his life.

For Gordon, it was like the axe (his ministry and calling) was at the bottom of the sea. Lost. Gone. Finished. I remember the speaker speaking over and over to Gordon's heart about the lost axe.

Pick it up, pick it up, pick it up, your ministry is not finished.

Gordon, by God's grace, did pick up the ministry. That time was a revival moment. Gordon was back. Gordon was restored and revived and, just like Elijah, recovered.

Prayer

O Lord, show me how I can be a father.
Direct me to support, befriend and love.
Lord, may I be a father.
And may I be a son or daughter to somebody.
Lord, lead me.
Thank You.
Amen.

KEEP WATCH

When Paul had finished speaking, he knelt down with all of them and prayed. They all wept as they embraced him and kissed him.

Acts 20:36-37

Keep Watch Over Yourselves

At Miletus, Paul requested the elders of the church at Ephesus to come and meet him on this solemn farewell occasion (Acts 20:17). Paul speaks with great honesty, love, and warmth to the elders when gathered. He thought he would not see them again, although in fact he did, and so he spoke accordingly. He spoke as a loving father to his little daughter. With tenderness.

Paul reminds the elders that he had not hesitated to preach on matters that would be helpful and relevant. Speaking with humility and tears. Paul reminded the elders that speaking to them was difficult because he was severely tested by the plots of the Jews who wanted to harm him or kill him. Sometimes we are called to minister while we are facing outside conflicts or inner personal distress, heartache, or injury.

Paul reminded the elders about what was important, issues of repentance and faith, and to focus on Jesus. Not all leaders, ministers, or evangelists do that today. Only faith in Jesus and His cross is needed to have eternal life. Good deeds or works do not earn an eternal destiny with God. I do not hear these truths often in churches. I do not hear about hell or Jesus's second coming. Some churches, along with many denominations, are full of people who do not know if they are going to heaven. Paul preached the word *(logos)* and the *now word* of God by the Holy Spirit *(rhema)*.

Keep Watch Over the Flock

Paul told the elders he had been governed by the Holy Spirit towards them. He reminded them of his sufferings, the riots, imprisonments, and beatings, but he was determined to finish the task. Paul told the elders to be focused on the Kingdom of God. Some leaders are focused on the church. The best leaders are focused on the Kingdom. Thy kingdom come. Paul did not hesitate to proclaim the whole will (counsel) of God to them. Paul gives the elders some final words and instructions:

- Keep watch over yourselves

- Guard the flock

- Shepherd the church of God

- Protect the church

- False teaching will arise from within

- Help the weak: 'It is more blessed to give than to receive'

- I worked hard while I was with you

- I never wanted anyone's money or clothing

- I did not take advantage or abuse you for my gain

When Paul finished speaking, he knelt down with all the elders and prayed. They began to weep aloud and embraced Paul. They repeatedly kissed him. They were especially sad because Paul had said he would not see them again. Paul was the father of the church. He brought them to Christ, discipled them, and planted the church at Ephesus.

My Story

I was a guest speaker over the weekend at a church. I was troubled in my spirit about the behaviour of its minister. I felt he was manipulating and spiritually abusing 'his' congregation.

In the evening, I preached but before doing that, I tried to give a warning to the minister during the church service, of how he should be. I spoke the word to the whole church in a manner that would be acceptable, focusing on the first and most important thing a pastor, or minister, or vicar, or any leader must do, *'keep watch over yourselves . . .' (*Acts 20:28).

This leader's behaviour was hurting people in his care. He was abusive. Leaders cannot pastor others with love unless they watch their own spirit. Abusive people are dangerous. The saying is true: 'Hurt people, hurt people.' Insecure people hurt people. Anyway, I gave the word and warning as best as I could. I do not think he listened. The minister continued his abusive behaviour. People suffered. The church crashed. A great church once upon a time. The Holy Spirit says to all of us, 'Listen if you have ears.'

Prayer

Good Shepherd, Lord Jesus.

Watch over Your church.

Help me, Jesus, to watch over my spirit and heart.

Fill us, Lord, with love and kind actions for Your people.

Father, guard me.

Holy Spirit, refresh me and renew me.

Thank You, Father.

Amen.

BOLD AS A LION

Leaving the next day, we reached Caesarea and stayed at the house of Philip the evangelist, one of the Seven. He had four unmarried daughters who prophesied.

Acts 21:8-9

Warnings on the Journey to Jerusalem

Paul sails from Ephesus arriving in Tyre, then Ptolemais, and finally Caesarea. In Caesarea, Paul stayed at the house of Philip the evangelist. Philip had four unmarried daughters who prophesied. These women may have dedicated themselves in a special way to serve the Lord and that is why they were unmarried. Perhaps they remained unmarried. We do not know.

Sometimes, a Christian sees their life being unmarried as a way of being able to serve the Lord more freely. Some widows, or widowers, or divorced Christians, decide not to marry for the same reason. To serve the Lord. Paul gives advice (it is not a command) as to being married or not in connection with serving the Lord. It is godly advice. His suggestion is worthy of prayerful consideration. Paul writes:

> *I would like you to be free from concern. An unmarried man is concerned about the Lord's affairs – how he can please the Lord. But a married man is concerned about the affairs of this world – how he can please his wife – and his interests are divided. An unmarried woman or virgin is concerned about the Lord's affairs: her aim is to be devoted to the Lord in both body and spirit. But a married woman is concerned about the affairs of this world – how she can please her husband. I am saying this for your own good, not to restrict you, but that you may live in a right way in undivided devotion to the Lord.*
>
> *1 Corinthians 7:32-35*

We should not despise those who are unmarried. And we should not think anything less of those who are single. The Lord Jesus has His perfect will for each of His children. If you come from a Greek-Cypriot culture or background, like mine, not to be married and staying single is not a normal thing. To be like that could be seen as strange or funny. We need to stop judging others.

Philip the Evangelist

Philip the anointed evangelist with his wonderful daughters encouraged Paul. Paul, in his second empowering letter, says to Timothy:

> *But you, keep your head in all situations, endure hardship, do the work of an evangelist, discharge all the duties of your ministry.*
>
> *2 Timothy 4:5*

Timothy's primary gifting and calling was that of a pastor or minister. But Paul charges Timothy to do the work of an evangelist. I believe all church ministers can do the work of an evangelist. Although my primary gifting is that of an evangelist, the Lord's word to me often is to do the work of a pastor. Was Paul an apostle? Was he a pastor? Was Paul an evangelist? Yes, to all. Paul majored on some and minored on other activity and gifting.

Christ Himself calls and appoints evangelists to His church. These are the gifts Christ gives His church: apostles, prophets, evangelists, pastors, and teachers (Ephesians 4:11). Some churches could have full-time evangelists on their staff, but they do not. Thank God I was on the staff of a church as its full-time evangelist for 10 years. The vicar had a pioneering vision, all those years ago, to appoint me. There was great fruit from this union.

Agabus the Prophet

Agabus the prophet prophesied over Paul in Caesarea. Agabus took Paul's belt, tied his own hands and feet with it and said:

> *The Holy Spirit declares, 'So shall the owner of this belt be bound by the Jewish leaders in Jerusalem and turned over to the Romans.'*
>
> *Acts 21:11 (NLT)*

Paul responded by assuring the Christians that he was willing to die for Jesus. Paul rejected pleas not to go to Jerusalem. Paul knew the prophetic word from the prophet Agabus was true, but the word needed to be interpreted correctly. In the end it was.

Paul travels to Jerusalem from Caesarea accompanied by his friends. Paul attends the temple. Here, a mob of religious people turns against Paul, falsely accusing him of teaching against the Jewish laws and commandments, the people of Israel, and defiling the temple. Paul was dragged out of the temple and they tried to kill him.

The Roman commander sent soldiers to rescue Paul and they carry him away on their shoulders to safety. Paul is bold as a lion. Paul asks for permission to speak to the crowd. The crowd is silenced as Paul addresses the crowd in their own language, Aramaic.

Prayer

Lord, make me bold as a lion.

Not to fear anything or anyone.

Lord, please help me to speak out and to speak up.

To speak for You.

Lord, please speak to me and through me.

Thank You, Father God.

Amen.

REVIVAL CAUSES A REACTION
OR RESPONSE

The crowd listened until Paul said that word. Then they all began to shout, 'Away with such a fellow! He isn't fit to live!'

Acts 22:22 (NLT)

Paul Speaks Boldly to the Crowd

Paul addresses the Jerusalem mob in the temple. His word has been safely preserved for us in just 21 verses (Acts 22: 1–21). Paul gives his testimony of his persecution against the Christian church of God. The crowd would have really liked that. Paul spoke of how zealous and religious he was to obey their Jewish laws and customs. The crowd loved to hear that. Paul told them how he was a Jew and educated in their city Jerusalem. The crowd loved to hear that. Paul spoke to them with respect and in their language of Aramaic and that was proper. They also liked that.

Paul now tells the crowd that the Lord told him to leave Jerusalem because he was being sent far away to the Gentiles. The mob did not like that at all. The Jews thought of the Gentiles as dogs. In Middle Eastern culture, to call someone a dog is a derogative statement. The Bible says:

> *The crowd listened until Paul said that word. Then they all began to shout, 'Away with such a fellow! He isn't fit to live!'*
>
> Acts 22:22 (NLT)

The crowd had enough. The specific point Paul made about offering the Gentiles salvation was too much for them. At best, Israel tolerated the Gentiles but usually they despised them and hated them. Gentiles were dogs. The crowd believed Israel and its people were the only true religion. The fact that Paul was offering life (and eternal life) with his preaching to non-Jewish Gentiles was too much for their ears.

Paul did not pull back from speaking the truth. Paul was directed by the Lord on what to proclaim. Paul spoke in love. Paul was rejected harshly. We speak the truth only if we know the truth. We speak the truth by the Holy Spirit. The word of God is the truth. The words of Jesus are true. Only when we are controlled by the Holy Spirit and not by the sinful nature can we speak the truth with wisdom.

Controlled by Your Emotions

George Verwer spoke at one of our breakfast meetings. The Lord uses George in amazing ways. I read his book *The Revolution of Love* when I was a young Christian. It still speaks to me. George and I wrote to each other recently. He writes in his book about an incident that occurred in their work some years ago:

A team member made a mistake when doing something practical. Naturally, one of his colleagues was keen to put him right. Very quickly he said, 'This is wrong. You should have not done it that way.' The first team member said defensively, 'Well, I was told to do it that way.' The second, even more heatedly, said, 'Well, I know it is not right. This is what you should have done.' And soon they had a full-scale argument.

Later, I was able to have a talk with one who claimed to be right. I said to him, 'Do you still feel you were right in that situation?' 'Absolutely,' he said. 'I was right and everybody else knows I was right!' And, indeed, he had managed to convince everyone else that he was right – not only on the practical point but in the way he acted.

Then I said, 'Tell me, when you spoke to him, were you controlled by the Holy Spirit or by your emotions?' He stopped at that and thought for a minute. 'Well, I don't suppose that was really what you would call controlled by the Holy Spirit.'

I said, 'Well, then, you were controlled by your emotions.' He was a bit hesitant but said, 'All right, I admit that I was controlled by my emotions and not by the Holy Spirit, but I was still right.' So, I said, 'But surely the Word of God says those who are controlled by their sinful nature cannot please God!' (Romans 8:8).[5]

Nothing good comes out of the sinful nature. Those who are under the control of their sinful nature can never please God. Paul was controlled by the Holy Spirit, speaking the truth in love. You and I can do the same. Paul let people feel the weight of who he was. And Paul let them deal with it.

Follow the Spirit

Our church leaders, our government, the world system, our spouses, our children, our friends, our enemies, and all people need us to speak the truth to them. Dare we? Speaking to oppose, encourage, challenge, admonish, correct, inspire, and inform. We also need to speak about the Truth. That is, Jesus. It does not matter if people like it or not. The fear of a man is a snare (Proverbs 29:25). It does not matter if the outcome is not positive, speak anyway. It does not matter if it is not popular. Speak. It does not matter if we speak but lose. Speak. Speak the truth in love.

The commander is about to have Paul flogged when it is discovered that Paul is a Roman citizen. The commander frees Paul from his chains and he is not whipped. Paul is now in front of the religious high council defending his life. Paul is fearless. He knows his life is in God's hands.

Prayer of Trust in God

Unto thee, O LORD, do I lift up my soul.

O my God, I trust in thee: let me not be ashamed, let not mine enemies triumph over me.

Yea, let none that wait on thee be ashamed: let them be ashamed which transgress without cause.

Shew me thy ways, O LORD; teach me thy paths.

Lead me in thy truth, and teach me: for thou art the God of my salvation; on thee do I wait all the day.

Amen.

(Psalm 25:1-5 KJV)

Be Encouraged

The following night the Lord stood near Paul and said, 'Take courage! As you have testified about me in Jerusalem, so you must also testify in Rome.'

Acts 23:11

Paul Before the Sanhedrin

The Roman commander ordered the chief priests and Sanhedrin to assemble. The commander wanted to find out what the trouble was all about. The commander gave Paul the opportunity and freedom to address the large gathering.

Paul speaks about the resurrection of the dead to the crowd. He knew that this would 'set the cat amongst the pigeons'. The Pharisees and Sadducees in front of Paul disagreed violently about this doctrine. Paul divided the crowd's opinion about him. The Pharisees stood up and supported Paul. *'We find nothing wrong with this man'* (Acts 23:9). Others wanted to kill him.

The dispute became so violent that the commander was afraid Paul would be killed by the angry mob. Paul was taken to safety into the Roman barracks. That night, the Lord Jesus appeared to Paul and said,

> *Take courage! As you have testified about me in Jerusalem, so you must also testify in Rome.*
>
> *Acts 23:11*

The Plan to Kill Paul

More than 40 men swore an oath amongst themselves to kill Paul. They inform the chief priests, elders, and Sanhedrin, asking for their assistance. However, the Roman commander hears about this secret mission and acts to save Paul. The commander orders immediately 200 soldiers, 200 spearmen and 70 horsemen to take Paul at night to Caesarea to Felix the governor.

These 470 men protected Paul, the Roman citizen. The Roman commander wrote an official letter to Felix stating Paul's innocence and asking for his assistance. Paul arrives in Caesarea under the protection of Rome and God. Felix keeps Paul under guard in Herod's palace until the trial.

The Lord Jesus Stands Near

In times of crisis, Paul was given help. On this occasion Jesus speaks to Paul and tells him to *'be encouraged'*. Paul could indeed take courage because Jesus is on his side. Paul has the support and presence and love of Jesus. That is great. Paul knows he has God Almighty, Jesus Christ, and the Holy Spirit. All three never leave Paul, even in severe troubles. Paul feels God's presence. Paul is convinced that nothing can separate him from God's love. Paul says in his letter to the Christians in Rome:

For I am convinced that neither death nor life, neither angels nor demons, neither the present nor the future, nor any powers, neither height nor depth, nor anything else in all creation, will be able to separate us from the love of God that is in Christ Jesus our Lord.

Romans 8:38-39

We are not immune from trouble. Sometimes God removes us from trouble and other times helps us through it (Psalm 16:1). Paul had a divine preservation order on his life. He could not die until his allotted time by God Almighty. Paul's time on this earth was not up yet. God had things for him to do. Paul must go to Rome by divine decree. Nothing stopped him. Once in Rome, Paul ministers for a little longer in amazing ways.

ACCUSATIONS

When two years had passed, Felix was succeeded by Porcius Festus, but because Felix wanted to grant a favour to the Jews, he left Paul in prison.

Acts 24:27

The Accusations Against Paul

Antonius Felix was appointed Roman governor of Judea in AD52. Felix was originally a slave who was freed and was a high official in government when Paul was brought before him for trial (Acts 24).

Tertullus, a lawyer and capable orator, presented his case before Felix with Paul present. Tertullus accused Paul of being a plague – that is, a dangerous nuisance or troublemaker – stirring up riots among the Jews everywhere. Tertullus accused Paul of being the ringleader of the Nazarene sect (the Christians) who tried to desecrate the temple. A 'Nazarene' is simply a person that does not hold to the ancient truths and is strange. Others supported these accusations as being true.

Today, should God's servants dare to speak Bible truths, they will sooner or later face opposition and trouble. But if we change the authentic gospel, or Jesus, or Bible truths, to line up with the world's beliefs and system, then society and people will like it. However, we cannot compromise the truth. The world is squeezing the church and our freedoms. This pressure will intensify and increase.

Christian, if you speak out your convictions, soon you will be hounded or branded. Live a godly life and you will not escape persecution. Say nothing, do nothing and you will be 'safe'. The true Christian who shines and speaks out will suffer both from within the church and the world. Paul spoke out and was hounded and branded as a ringleader of the sect of the Nazarenes.

In his day, John Wesley, who brought God's revival, was hounded and branded by the church itself. John Wesley was thrown out of churches after he spoke and told to never return to preach. That is when Wesley took to the open air, speaking to hundreds and thousands. However, even then he suffered persecution many times. But thousands were converted as Wesley proclaimed the truth of the gospel. The liberal gospel has nothing to offer. The authentic gospel is the power of God to save people's souls and give eternal life (Romans 1:16).

Paul is requested by Felix to defend himself and put his case forward. Paul deals excellently with every false accusation against him. Felix adjourned the proceedings and gave orders to the centurion to keep Paul under guard, but he was allowed some freedom. Paul's friends were permitted to take care of his needs.

Inconvenient to Change

Felix and his wife Drusilla liked to listen to Paul who spoke frequently to them on righteousness, self-control, and judgement to come. Felix would become afraid and send Paul away. Pride, selfish ambitions, and sin made it inconvenient for Felix to change. Felix was hoping Paul would pay him a bribe for release, but Paul never did.

Felix did not want to face the fierce anger of the Jews so would not release Paul. Paul was held in prison for two years. Felix was recalled to Rome in AD59/60 to answer for irregularities in his rule, such as handling of riots between the Jewish and Syrian inhabitants and other disturbances. Felix was weak, self-centred, and was protecting himself from both his superiors and those he ruled. Consequently, he did not bring justice in the case of Paul but did nothing instead. However, even that was God's providence because Paul had freedom to continue his ministry within prison. God preserved Paul.

YOUR STORY

When Paul came in, the Jews who had come down from Jerusalem stood around him. They brought many serious charges against him, but they could not prove them.

Acts 25:7

Then I asked, 'Who are you, Lord?' 'I am Jesus, whom you are persecuting,' the Lord replied.

Acts 26:15

God Guides Paul

Porcius Festus was appointed governor in the place of Felix. There was still pressure from the religious leaders for Paul to be tried and the Jews requested for the trial to be carried out in Jerusalem. They wanted to ambush the travelling party from Caesarea to Jerusalem. Festus asks Paul if he would give his consent to be tried in Jerusalem, but Paul declined, stating he wanted to be tried before Caesar's court. Paul, a Roman citizen, had full rights to be tried in Rome in the civil court by Caesar. Festus granted Paul's request.

King Agrippa visits Festus one day and Festus gives him a brief account of the matter between Paul and the Jews. Festus felt and told the king that Paul had done nothing wrong to deserve death. Festus tells the king that he has nothing definite to write about Paul to the Emperor. Festus felt it was unreasonable to send a prisoner without specifying the charges against him. Festus sought King Agrippa's advice and assistance.

King Agrippa gives Paul permission to speak (Acts 26). Once King Agrippa hears apostle Paul's defence and story, he tells Festus that the accused has not done anything that deserves death or imprisonment, adding that Paul could have been set free if Paul had not appealed to Caesar.

Paul's Account of His Conversion

Paul tells his story to the king, his wife Bernice, Festus, and many others (Acts 26:1-32). Paul gives his testimony before his conversion (BC), his actual conversion (C), and after his conversion (AC). There are two things the Lord uses when we speak to those in the world who do not know Jesus: the gospel and our story. Paul speaks about his life **before conversion:**

- Jewish religious training from earliest childhood
- Lived among his people and in Jerusalem
- Strict Pharisee
- Opposed the name of Jesus
- Put Christians in prison
- Persecuted Christians in foreign cities
- Believed the Messiah was coming

Having explained something of his life before his amazing conversion to Jesus, he begins to talk about his **conversion**:

- On a mission to persecute more Christians
- At noon, blinded by light
- Hears Jesus speak, 'Why do you persecute me?'
- Jesus commissions him to speak to Jews and Gentiles about Jesus's forgiveness

Having explained something of the facts of his conversion (Acts 26:12-18), Paul begins to tell King Agrippa about his life **after conversion**:

- Become obedient to Jesus's vision
- Proclaimed Christ: Damascus, Jerusalem and Judea
- Proclaimed Christ: Gentiles
- Preached Christ died for sins
- Preached Christ rose from the dead

Having heard Paul's story, King Agrippa stops Paul speaking and says, '*Do you think you can make me a Christian so quickly?*' (Acts 26:28 NLT). Paul is happy that everyone in the audience has heard about Jesus and His transforming power. Paul certainly believes it is indeed possible for the king and anyone else present to become a Christian.

Before Conversion, Conversion, After Conversion

My own conversion story has a before conversion, conversion (summer of 1973), and what happened after my conversion until now. Before conversion I went to church from the age of six years. I prayed to God but did not know Him at all. I believed

Christianity was a waste of time. I was a thief and stole from people, shops, and school. I was happy and was embarking on an engineering career.

Suddenly, without looking for Jesus, for some strange reason I attended a Christian camp. I was converted one night. I shocked myself at the decision. The next year I was baptised in the Holy Spirit. I have boldness to not only tell others of Jesus, but many became Christians. The stealing stopped. My life began to be transformed. Jesus is real. Jesus is close and became a friend.

Today I am blessed with the privilege of sharing the Good News in the United Kingdom and have ministered in countries in Europe and Africa. I want others to know Jesus, have sins forgiven, experience His transforming power, get a fresh start, and have eternal life. Even though we all have difficulties, stresses, and problems, it is still a life in all its fullness. Jesus makes the difference.

Prayer

Oh Lord Jesus.
I have a story to tell.
Help me to share it.
To share what You have done for me.
To allow You to speak to others through my story, Lord.
Thank You, Jesus.
Amen.

HOPE

When neither sun nor stars appeared for many days and the storm continued raging, we finally gave up all hope of being saved.

Acts 27:20

Sailing to Rome

Paul joined other prisoners and boarded a ship with soldiers and a centurion named Julius (Acts 27). The ship sailed from Caesarea in a northerly direction, passing around the tip of Cyprus, landing at Myra in Lycia. In Myra they boarded an Alexandrian ship which was bound for Rome. From Myra the ship sailed to Fair Havens on the Island of Crete. Today Crete is a Greek island (and I have enjoyed a wonderful holiday there). Here Paul warns the centurion that the voyage is going to be disastrous with loss of the ship and cargo, but the centurion did not listen to the apostle or wait for good weather.

The ship continued its journey, leaving the Island of Crete and passing the small Island of Cauda. But now they were experiencing hurricane-force winds. The ship managed at this point to continue its dangerous journey but had to throw away cargo because the ship was being battered by the storm. As they continue, they throw out the ship's equipment and anything they could lay their hands on. The terrible storm raged continually for many days until at last all hope was gone.

Everyone except Paul had finally given up all hope of being saved. Hope was gone. Paul speaks again to everyone saying that not one of the 276 men on board would be lost but the ship would be destroyed. He told the men that he was on a divine mission to arrive in Rome to stand trial before Caesar. Therefore, he and everyone would live. Paul urged the men to keep their courage, that he trusted God for safety. He told the men the ship would run aground on some island. The bold apostle and prophet had spoken.

Surviving the Storm

If we listen to the Lord and trust His word, we are safe even when things are difficult or tragic. Christian hope is different from the hope the world offers. The world's hope is, 'Well I hope my football club wins against Arsenal. Perhaps they will, perhaps they will not.' The world's hope cannot be compared with Christian hope. Christian hope brings revival. Christian hope is like faith. Paul had hope, a certainty, a faith. But the Bible says at one point the men on the ship, battered by violent winds, finally gave up all hope of being saved (Acts 27:20).

There have been times when I almost lost all hope of God rescuing me from perilous situations. The wind and the storms against me seemed almost too much. Times when I was shipwrecked by circumstances. By God's grace and mercy there was always at least a little faith and hope. Faith that my Jesus would bring me through. Jesus did. He has. He will.

Shipwreck

Everybody on the ship was told by Paul to eat. He was concerned for them. As they approached the Island of Malta, the ship struck a sandbar and ran aground. The stern was repeatedly smashed by the force of the waves and began to break apart. The commanding officer ordered all who could swim to jump overboard and make for land. The others held to the planks and debris from the broken ship. Everyone escaped to safety on the beach on the Island of Malta.

Put your hope in God. Your hope comes from the Lord (Psalm 62:5). Put your hope in God's word. There is surely a future hope for you; God's plans for you come with hope and a future (Jeremiah 29:11). We wait for the blessed hope (Titus 2:13). We have this hope as an anchor (Hebrews 6:19). Hope deferred makes the heart sick. The fruit of the Holy Spirit produces hope.

UNHINDERED

He proclaimed the kingdom of God and taught about the Lord Jesus Christ – with all boldness and without hindrance!

Acts 28:31

Revival in Malta

Paul and the hundreds that were on the ship are now saved, having reached the shore of the Island of Malta. The islanders showed great kindness by building a fire to warm them and welcome them. Paul went to Publius's home in Malta. Publius was the chief official of the Island. Paul placed his hands on Publius's mother who was sick with fever and dysentery. She was healed.

That was another reason for the shipwreck. For Paul to arrive and bring healing and salvation. Then all the other sick people on the island came and were cured. Paul was waiting for three months for the next Alexandrian ship to Rome to arrive.

Freedom in Rome

Paul arrives in Rome. He was permitted to have his own private lodging, although he was guarded by a soldier. After just three days in Rome, Paul calls local Jewish leaders to get acquainted, to tell them about the hope of Israel. To tell them that the Messiah, Jesus, has already come. Paul told many people about the Kingdom of God. He taught them about Jesus from the five books of Moses and the books of the prophets. Paul would lecture in the morning into the evening. Some believed and some did not.

Revival Followed Paul

For two years, Paul lived in his own rented house. He welcomed all who visited Him. He focused his teaching on the Kingdom of God with much boldness and taught about the Lord Jesus Christ. He had freedom; no one tried to stop him. While Paul was waiting for his accusers to press for the trial in Rome, he served the Lord and ministered. This was Paul's third missionary journey, from AD53–57.

Paul declared his intention to go to Spain (Romans 15:24, 28). It could be that Paul was released following his first Roman imprisonment. We do not know for sure, but it is a possibility with good reasons, that Paul carried out a fourth missionary journey in AD62–67/68 (this could have been Spain) and returned to Rome. Paul may have been martyred in AD67/68.

Giant

Paul was a giant. A bold man who loved Jesus more than anything or anybody. He was willing to die for Jesus at any time. Paul was humble as he sometimes worked his tent-making business to give himself support to function as a missionary. Paul worked not to be a burden to the church. Unlike today where many are pastors (America, Nigeria) because it is a business opportunity, and money can be extracted from congregations.

Paul had a huge impact by spreading the gospel in towns and cities in Europe. People became followers of Jesus. Paul made disciples by God's revival power. He planted churches, established elders, and had assistants and worked in teams. Paul trained others. Paul was not afraid to challenge, correct, rebuke, or encourage. When the church was wrong in its ways or teaching, he would not allow it to carry on in those ways. Where is that Spirit of Jesus in God's ministers today?

Prayer

Lord, Paul had Your Holy Spirit.
O, Lord, grant me Your revival Spirit.
Lord, make me bold and compassionate.
Lord, here I am,
Send me, use me, keep me.
In Jesus's name.
Amen.

DESIRE

When he heard that it was Jesus of Nazareth, he began to shout, 'Jesus, Son of David, have mercy on me!'

Mark 10:47

Blind Bartimaeus was sitting begging by the roadside when he heard Jesus was close by with His disciples and a large crowd (Mark 10:46-52). Bartimaeus was a despised beggar. A rejected man. I have seen many men like this by the roadside in Nigeria. When Bartimaeus hears Jesus is close by, he cries out, *'Jesus, Son of David, have mercy on me.'*

The crowd told him to shut up. His desire is very strong and so Bartimaeus cries out to Jesus again. Jesus stops. The Saviour asks Bartimaeus what he wants. He simply says that he wants to see.

Desire for the Holy Spirit

We receive from the Lord only as much as we really want. My friend Revd Anthony Chamberlain has written one of the best books I have read. It is called, *The Promise of the Father.* It is a timely message. Here are two extracts with his helpful table about the Holy Spirit.

One of John Wesley's students commented that he would like to receive a particular gift of the Holy Spirit. Wesley took him to the washroom and asked him to pour a good amount of water into the basin. This done, Wesley pushed the student's face into the water and held him there until he thrashed wildly. Releasing him, Wesley said, 'When you want a gift of the Spirit as much as you wanted air, you will get it.'[6]

There is ample evidence of the manifestations (gifts) of the Spirit in use within the church down the centuries. For example, Augustine in the fourth century wrote, 'We still do what the apostles did when they laid hands on the converts to receive the Holy Spirit. It is expected that the converts will speak in tongues.'[7]

BEING OUR BEST FOR GOD[8]

Not Baptised in the Holy Spirit
No Bible Study and Weak Faith

This person attends church, but they are not baptised in the Holy Spirit. They rarely study or prepare for God's service. God is restricted by their lack of dedication.

Effectiveness: 20%

Baptised in the Holy Spirit
No Bible Study and Weak Faith

This person is baptised in water and baptised in the Holy Spirit. They rely on the Spirit for guidance, but rarely study the Bible, and the Spirit finds difficulty in using them.

Effectiveness: 40%

Not Baptised in the Holy Spirit
Studies Bible and Believes God

This person is saved, but not baptised in the Holy Spirit. Continually they study the Bible and pray for God to use them. They are better material for the Spirit's ministry.

Effectiveness: 70%

Baptised in the Holy Spirit
Studies Bible and Believes God

This person is saved, baptised in water and in the Holy Spirit. They seek God daily to be filled. They avidly study the Bible, pray and trust God to use them powerfully for His glory.

Effectiveness: 100%

LETTING GO

Therefore, there is now no condemnation for those who are in Christ Jesus.

Romans 8:1

Auschwitz 1944

It is 1944 and sixteen-year-old ballerina Edith Eger is sent to Auschwitz. Separated from her parents on arrival, she endures unimaginable experiences, including being made to dance for the infamous Josef Mengele. When the camp is finally liberated, she is pulled from a pile of bodies, barely alive.

The horrors of the Holocaust did not break Edith. In fact, they helped her learn to live again with a life-affirming strength and a truly remarkable resilience. The book The Choice is her unforgettable story. It shows that hope can flower in the most unlikely places.

Edith Eger is with her mother and sister in Auschwitz in line with hundreds of others waiting for their fate. Dr Mengele is deciding which people go to the left, and which go to the right. One side means execution by gas, and the other side prison and life. Dr Mengele asks little Edith who the person near is and whether it is her older sister or mother. Edith does not fully know or understand what is going on. She answers that it is her mother. Edith does not know at that moment that her answer will send her mother to the gas chamber, along with many others.

Letting Go

Many years after the war, Edith returned to Auschwitz to deal with her past. During her visit to Auschwitz many thoughts went through her mind as she sought further peace and healing within. Edith writes that if she had known her mother would be sent to the gas chamber, she would have given a different answer or said nothing at all to Mengele. She feels perhaps she could have followed her mother to the gas chamber and died with her. She wonders if she could have done something different. She believes she could have done more.

Edith realises that it is fantasy to believe we are in control. She rebukes herself for making the wrong choice. But she was too young, terrified, vulnerable, and had only one second to decide. Today Edith knows that she can make more important choices. To accept herself as she is. To stop asking herself, 'Why did I survive?' To realise she can be helpful in serving others because of her own trauma, loss, and struggle. The greatest thing Edith does for herself is to stop running from the past. To let it go. She makes that choice.

We need to forgive ourselves. When we confess our sins, God is faithful (He keeps His promise to forgive), and is just (He does the right thing), and will forgive us from all and every sin (1 John 1:9).

Stop judging yourself. Therefore, there is now no condemnation because of what Jesus has done for you. For me.

The Choice

Edith Eger was freed from Auschwitz and became a psychologist, author, and international speaker. She has helped individuals to freedom from their own mental prisons. She has taken her liberating message to thousands of people. Her book, The Choice, is a book for all to read. Indeed, we have a choice.

To let others decide for you is to be passive. When we are aggressive to others, we decide for them. Deciding for yourself requires you to be assertive. Learning to trust yourself is necessary.

Edith Eger in America

Eger emigrated to America years after Auschwitz and in her book describes a day when she worked in the office of a luggage company. Her boss was Jewish, and she hoped she would at last do well there. One day, the telephone was ringing and there was no one in the office able to answer. Edith picked up the telephone but her boss burst out of his office and began shouting at Edith for answering the telephone. He told Edith not to ruin the company and its reputation. It was verbal abuse.

Edith was not concerned about the abusive and horrible things her boss said to her, but the problem was she believed her boss's assessment of her worthlessness. The hardest part of healing is to accept yourself. To be happy with yourself. We do not need to make up for our brokenness with achievements, awards, degrees, or fame. None of these things fix us. Edith has discovered this.

Dr Edith Eger's therapy could be called 'Choice Therapy.' Freedom is about choice. Where the Holy Spirit of the Lord is, there is freedom. Choose forgiveness, compassion, and faith. Edith Eger's therapy is about not being stuck in the past but living in the present. We destroy ourselves when we live in the past. We hurt ourselves when we keep saying 'if only': 'If only I did not do what I did,' 'If only I married a different person,' 'If only I had spoken out sooner.'

However, we could also spend time in the future saying, 'I will only be happy when I have plenty of money' or 'I will only be happy when I meet the right person.'

It is for freedom that Christ has set us free. Stand firm, then, and do not let yourselves be burdened again by a yoke of slavery.
Galatians 5:1

ABUSE

His talk is smooth as butter, yet war is in his heart; his words are more soothing than oil, yet they are drawn swords.

Psalm 55:21

Emotional and Verbal Abuse

All abuse – whether it is emotional, verbal, mental, physical, spiritual, or sexual – damages people. Any kind of abuse wounds the heart or spirit. This is a true statement:

The human spirit can endure a sick body, but who can bear it if the spirit is crushed?

Proverbs 18:14 (NLT)

Emotional abuse is any ongoing, negative behaviour used to control or hurt another person.

Verbal abuse is the regular and ongoing use of harmful words or sharp tone in an attempt to control, or dominate, and hurt another person. Mistreatment that is ongoing is abusive. To abuse someone brings destruction. Emotional and verbal abuse more than just hurt the feeling of others, which is bad enough, but

147

it is destructive. It seems to me that the world sees verbal and emotional abuse more clearly than many Christians and churches. The world understands well the big effects and damage caused by abuse.

All day long you plot destruction. Your tongue cuts like a sharp razor; you're an expert at telling lies.

Psalm 52:2 (NLT)

The tongue can cut deep. There is a children's rhyme that says, 'Sticks and stones may break my bones, but words may never hurt me.' That rhyme is rubbish. The rhyme about words is a lie. Most, if not all of us, have experienced the truth that the tongue can cut deep, bringing abuse, hurt, and damage.

The Abusive Spirit

The fruit or actions of an abusive spirit is what the sinful nature produces (Galatians 5:20-21):

- Hatred
- Discord
- Jealousy
- Fits of rage
- Selfish ambition
- Dissensions
- Factions
- Envy

The fruit of the Holy Spirit is love, joy, peace, patience, kindness, goodness, faithfulness, gentleness, and self-control (Galatians 5:22-23). When we allow the Holy Spirit to have His way through us, we are compassionate and loving and not abusive. If we allow the sinful nature to manifest or control us, we can become abusive.

Abusers and Victims

Abusers have wrong convictions about their (abusive) behaviour when they believe they are not responsible for the way they treat others. Abusers believe others are to blame for their actions upon their victims. Abusers have the right belief about themselves when they admit they are in fact responsible for the way they have acted on others (the victims).

Victims have the wrong convictions about themselves when they hold themselves responsible for the way others (the abusers) have treated them. Victims feel they are to blame, they are bad. Victims have the right convictions about themselves when they realise they are not to blame themselves for being treated wrongly by others.

Those who have been verbally and emotionally abused can confront their abusers. Setting boundaries is absolutely necessary. It is again vital we learn to say 'no' to abuse. It is vital to be assertive. It is confronting for change.

Know this, you cannot negotiate with the devil. Jesus does not. In other words, do not negotiate with someone who is abusive (and that is the way they are going to stay). Do not think you can make peace with abuse. Sometimes it is best to run. Remove yourself. I resigned from my job years ago because abuse was present. Put your trust in God. Do not rely on people. It is difficult to find people of wisdom to advise you when it comes to abusive situations. But pray and let God guide you.

Winston Churchill said about trying to negotiate peace with Adolf Hitler and Nazi Germany, 'There shall be no negotiated peace.'

Almost everyone was pressing Winston Churchill to make peace. But Winston discerned and understood the evil heart of Hitler. Hitler the abuser, and evil man.

BOUNDARIES

Fearing people is a dangerous trap, but trusting the LORD means safety.

Proverbs 29:25 (NLT)

Setting Boundaries

For proper living, we need to set boundaries and keep them. Years ago, I worked in an organisation and enjoyed it greatly. As part of my work, I had regular staff meetings. We talked about how things were progressing and planned for the future. However, the situation within the organisation had deteriorated and I, along with others, were affected. I felt my boss was behaving inappropriately towards me. Although I spoke to him about it, there was no improvement. I felt unsafe.

One day, I remember it well, I attended a meeting having decided about putting a boundary in place. I told my boss that I did not want to meet with him for any further meetings where it was just me and him. I requested another person to be present in future meetings. My boss did not think that was necessary. He did not like my suggestion. I put a boundary in place for my safety and well-being. From then on, every time we had a staff meeting with my boss, someone else was present.

Boundaries are needed for daily life. They are indispensable and often exist unnoticed. There are personal boundaries, physical boundaries, and spiritual boundaries. Boundaries have established limits and dividing lines. Personal boundaries give protection.

Personal Boundaries Bring Freedom

Personal boundaries allow you to arrange what belongs to you and what belongs to someone else. Boundaries allow you to show to others how you will maintain control over your body, mind, and Christian convictions. Boundaries let you set limits in your relationships and your right to enforce them. They allow you to decide what your unique gifts and assignments are that align with your calling with Jesus. We cannot be persuaded to do something that brings chaos in our lives. Personal boundaries produce order and life.

Personal boundaries communicate and show others what you will endure and will not endure. These boundaries say what you will or will not accept. Boundaries convey what your values are, what you believe and what you do not. These boundaries speak of what essentially you are, and what you are not.

We need wisdom to set very good boundaries. Prayer will help to find out what the best boundaries are for us in our relationships and work situations.

Good Boundaries and Fear

When we face certain situations about what is said or done to us, we need to respond. We do so by exercising good or bad boundaries. We can apply bad boundaries (or no boundaries) if we are afraid to confront because we fear people. We may be afraid they will not agree with us. Silence is sometimes a poor boundary. Exercising a good boundary means we are not afraid to confront, kindly but firmly. We do this trusting that the Lord is leading us to do the right thing. It is dangerous to be concerned with what others think of you.

No Consequence

We all experience bad behaviour in our relationships. At times we need to set a boundary with consequences. If we do not set out the consequences for hurt caused, the offender may repeat the hurt. We may be mistaken to think this person will not continue causing pain. If the hurting person is an untrustworthy character, then it is necessary to act accordingly.

Setting out a boundary that carries consequence for unacceptable behaviour is only any good if it is enforced. Should there be no change in the offending person, then you may need to discontinue the relationship. You can reward positive change of behaviour with encouraging words and appreciation; this may help the relationship to improve and progress.

Talk About Boundaries

In parenting you may say to your young teenager, 'If you choose to play football in the small back garden again (and not the park) and smash the glass windows, the repercussion is that I will remove the football from you and stop your pocket money for months.'

We communicate about boundaries in the workplace, marriage, friendships, school, in parenting, and everywhere where there are people. We need to state our needs, establish boundaries, and explain what acceptable and appropriate behaviour is and what it is not.

CONFRONTATION

A wise son heeds his father's instruction, but a mocker does not respond to rebukes.

Proverbs 13:1

Challenging Others for Change

Confrontation means facing up to and dealing with a problem or difficulty. Confrontation is about challenging others or a situation to change. Throughout my life I have noticed that some people seem to be able to confront others easily. I have observed good confrontation and bad confrontation. For myself, confrontation is not easy, but I see clearly that it is often necessary, and therefore I will confront.

One of my staff at our school in Nigeria admitted that he found confrontation impossible. He avoids it and cannot confront. This person is an excellent member of staff and I am delighted with his contribution to our ministry. But for his own sake, there is a time to confront.

My Father, Demetrakis (1933–1997)

My father, Demetrakis, took his fantastic new 320i BMW car to have its annual service at the garage. He knew the mechanic and felt he would do a good job. The car had a straight six-cylinder engine with fuel injection and held the road superbly. My father collected the car once the service was completed and drove it home. He felt he should check to see if all was well and the service was done perfectly. He carried out his examination and discovered the oil filter had not been changed, neither the oil, nor the spark plugs.

My father took the car back to this dishonest garage and confronted the person responsible. He told the garage owner he was a thief and a liar. My father did not want any money back and never used the service of that garage again. My father was in no doubt of the situation. He told us all what happened, but I wish I were there at the garage, to see him in action, when he confronted the mechanic.

We must not avoid confrontation when it is necessary. There is good and bad confrontation. There were times when my father did not do confrontation well. As a consequence, others suffered. We all sometimes get it wrong but that should not stop us from confronting. The Lord will help us to do so.

Do we confront when we should not? Do we avoid confronting when we should? The fear of conflict can make us passive and do nothing. We can confront inappropriately when we do not understand the situation, or we do not really know how to do so properly. Be careful, even when we confront properly, for the purpose of change, confrontation does not guarantee the right outcome. Jesus confronted. Sometimes His hearers changed, often they did not. Some turned against Jesus because they felt what He said and did was not to their liking.

When To and Not To Confront

We should confront when someone sins against us (Matthew 18:15), when division exists within a group (Romans 14:19), when someone is caught in a sin, when you are offended (Ephesians 4:2-3), when others are offended (Galatians 2:11-13), when a relationship is threatened (Philippians 4:2-3), when someone is in danger (Proverbs 24:11-12).

We should not confront when we are not the right person to confront, when it is not the right time, when we are uncertain of the facts, when it is better to overlook a minor offence, when we are committing the same sin (Matthew 7:3-5), when we have a vindictive attitude (Roman 12:17), when the person we want to confront has a habit of foolishness and quarrelling (2 Timothy 2:23-24), and perhaps when the confrontation will be ineffective and refusal severe (Proverbs 9:7).

However, with such a person we still need to have and apply proper boundaries. Again, we should not confront when our motive is only our own rights and not going to benefit the other person (Philippians 2:3-4) and when a person who offended us is our enemy (Matthew 5:44-45).

Sometimes people react with anger or defensively when confronted. Remember, we cannot control the response of others. Our part is to confront and allow others the opportunity to change lovingly and properly. Sometimes we must release people and leave them to God. If we have repeatedly confronted a situation or a person for change, but there is no change, we do not need to carry on confronting.

If anyone will not welcome you or listen to your words, leave that home or town and shake the dust off your feet.

Matthew 10:14

Confrontation That Is Positive

Positive confrontation looks at the behaviour, is hopeful, loving and encouraging, gives an opportunity for growth and become more like Jesus, gives the other person time (perhaps with limits), puts boundaries in place, gives clarity about the consequences if the situation does not change, offers forgiveness, and is calm. Confrontation for change is assertive, firm and yet kind.

Nelson Mandela confronted the oppressive apartheid system in South Africa. As a consequence, he was imprisoned for 27 years. Later he obtained freedom. I am learning to confront. It is one of the most vital necessities if we want to live fully and properly like Jesus.

Jesus confronted His own mother, disciples, dead religion, abuse of all kinds, wrong teaching of the priests and leaders, and bad behaviour towards children, women, and the poor.

Prayer

Lord, please confront me.

Do so with love.

Lord, help me confront others,

With love and firmness.

In Jesus's name. Amen.

Does Love Cover a Multitude of Sins?

Have nothing to do with the fruitless deeds of darkness, but rather expose them.

Ephesians 5:11

Jesus Rebukes Peter

Love rebukes. Jesus explains to His beloved disciples that He, the Christ, must be killed and rise again. The Bible says Peter, on hearing these words (Mark 8:31–33), takes Jesus to one side and then begins to rebuke Him. Peter has no conception of a suffering and rejected Messiah. I find it strange that Peter even thinks it is all right to rebuke Jesus on such a matter in the first place. It is not good for us nor is it acceptable to cast aside Jesus's words. Honestly, how can you or I rebuke Jesus?

Jesus respond to Peter saying, *'Get behind me, Satan. You do not have in mind the things of God, but the things of men.'* Because Jesus loves Peter, He rebukes Him. It is wrong to let some things go. True love rebukes with kindness.

159

Paul, writing to the believers at Corinth, tells them not to associate with anyone who claims to be Christian yet indulges in sexual sins, or is greedy, or worships idols, or is abusive, or a drunkard, or a swindler. Paul adds, do not even eat with such people (1 Corinthians 5:11). In other words, love does cover a multitude of sin but not all sins. If the true Christian has an intimate association with someone who does 'eat' with such people, the non-Christian world may assume that the church approves of such behaviour, and the name of Christ would be dishonoured.

If a Christian is overcome by some sin, we who are godly should gently and humbly help that person to restoration. And we should all be careful not to fall ourselves in like manner. That was Paul's encouragement to the Galatian Christians (Galatians 6:1).

James encourages us to restore a Christian who has wandered from the truth (James 5:19). Jesus says that when someone offends us deeply, we are to talk with them so that the relationship can be repaired (Matthew 18:15-17).

It is not possible to have a close relationship with anyone who repeatedly and seriously sins against us and is not willing to see what he or she has done or is doing wrong and not willing to change. Unconditional love does not mean unconditional relationship.

Neutrality

A relationship needs boundaries to be healthy and spiritually alive. Repeated destructive behaviour in a relationship from one person towards the other harms the friendship. Progress can only be achieved if the destructive person sees and owns up to the hurt they are causing. For counsellors trying to assist in such matters much wisdom is needed. For counsellors to act neutral in the matter only enables the person's self-deception to grow unchallenged. Sin hidden harms, but honesty means restoration (Proverbs 28:18).

It is not appropriate for counsellors or pastors to take a neutral position when having a face-to-face meeting with the perpetrator and victim. The effect of neutrality can be devastating.

Neutrality is not neutral. Neutrality effectively means you become an ally of the abuser, because by taking the view that both parties are contributing to a marriage problem, then you are effectively saying, 'It is not abuse.' This only serves the agender of the abuser.

Prayer

> *Lord Jesus, help me to be restored.*
> *Use my life to bring restoration.*
> *Encourage and rebuke me, Lord.*
> *Help me, Lord, to encourage and rebuke gently.*
> *Lord, when I am broken, heal me.*
> *May my life bring healing by Your Holy Spirit.*
> *Amen.*

HE HATES OR GOD HATES
(MALACHI 2:16)

'If he hates and divorces his wife,' says the LORD God of Israel, 'he covers his garment with injustice,' says the LORD of Hosts. Therefore, watch yourselves carefully, and do not act treacherously.'

Malachi 2:16 (CSB)

In Malachi's time, the ancient people of God, the Jewish people, the men, were acting treacherously towards the Lord and their wives (Malachi 2:10-17). The men had defiled the Lord's beloved sanctuary and laws by marrying women who worshipped idols. Such marriages between believers and nonbelievers (pagans) were forbidden. Such unions would lead to apostasy. The Lord spoke through the prophet Malachi to the men, telling them to guard their hearts and not to deal treacherously towards their wives.

Treacherous Divorce

The men were behaving *treacherously,* as the New King James Version of the Bible says, and this is mentioned again and again

(Malachi 2:10-16). The men hated their wives. This unloving and hurtful behaviour led the men in divorcing their wives. This was treacherous divorce.

> 'The man who hates and divorces his wife,' says the LORD, the God of Israel, 'does violence to the one he should protect,' says the LORD Almighty. So be on your guard, and do not be unfaithful.
>
> Malachi 2:16

The men were putting away their wives, divorcing them and thereby overwhelming the women with cruelty. Their husbands were covering their own lives with crime and sin.

Who is doing the hating in Malachi 2:16? It is not God. The text says, 'The man who hates and divorces.' God did not say 'I hate divorce' in Malachi. What the Lord through Malachi condemned was treacherous divorce. That is, the men who divorced their wives without righteous reason, such as adultery, but did so anyway because of hatred and aversion. Malachi and the Lord is saying nothing about disciplinary divorce in this passage.

Disciplinary Divorce

Disciplinary divorce could be for adultery, abuse, neglect, or desertion. Disciplinary divorce is not what Malachi is talking about and against. There are different forms of abuse. Abuse could be physical, sexual, financial, emotional, verbal, or spiritual.

God did not condemn *all* divorce in Malachi, nor did God say, 'I hate divorce.' We should stop using the phrase or motto, 'God hates divorce.' It will be biblically accurate to say, 'God does not hate disciplinary divorce, but does hate treacherous divorce.' It is a mistranslation to say, 'God hates divorce.' To use such a slogan when referring to yourself or others can cut like a knife, as if God hates all divorce. It is important that we are aware of the correct translation of Malachi and understand the context.

Divorce: Treacherous and Disciplinary

We need to understand the difference between disciplinary divorce, which is allowed, and treacherous divorce, which Malachi and the Lord were not pleased about. Jesus was, and is, against treacherous divorce. The Bible allows disciplinary divorce. Christianity (often) does not. Victims of divorce or marital abuse can suffer greatly, feel great fear and guilt if they believe God (and perhaps God's people) hates all divorce. Clarity about the meaning of Malachi is essential for well-being.

There are at least 18 scholars or sources that say, 'he hates . . . he covers', is the most faithful way to translate the Hebrew, with 'he' being the divorcing husband in Malachi 2:16. These are some of the translations taken from Barbara Roberts book *Not Under Bondage: Biblical Divorce for Abuse, Adultery and Desertion:*

- 1927 (J.M.P. Smith) *'For one who hates and divorces,' says the Lord God of Israel, 'covers his clothing with violence,' says the Lord of Hosts.*
- 1986 (Westbrook) *For he has hated, divorced . . . and covered his garment in injustice . . .*
- 1997 (Sprinkle) *When he hates so as to divorce, says the LORD God of Israel, then he covers himself with lawlessness.*
- 1998 (Stuart) *If one hates and divorces (Yahweh, Israel's God, said), he covers his clothes with crime (Yahweh of the Armies said).*

- 1999 (Shields) *For one who hates and divorces, says Yahweh, the God of Israel, covers his garment with violence, says almighty Yahweh.*

- 2001 (English Standard Version) *For the man who hates and divorces, says the Lord, covers his garment with violence, says the Lord of hosts.*[9]

Not Under Bondage

Barbara Roberts's helpful book *Not Under Bondage: Biblical Divorce for Abuse, Adultery, and Desertion* examines: abuse; Jesus's and apostle Paul's teaching; 1 Corinthians 7:10-16, and Malachi 2:16. Roberts answers questions such as: Does the apostle Paul permit divorce for an abused spouse? May I remarry if I have suffered divorce?, 'God hates divorce'– slogan or scripture?, Isn't adultery the ONLY ground for divorce?, If I am the innocent party, why do I feel guilty? Roberts concludes her book with her closing plea.

Closing Plea

If I could make one plea it would be that teachers and speakers evaluate what they plan to say by imagining how a victim of marital abuse would be likely to hear their message. Teachers need to ask themselves: 'How would a victim interpret my teaching? Is there anything in what I plan to say that would further entrap a person who is subordinated in an abusive marriage? Would they feel I have condemned and cut off their hope for freedom?' It takes only 11 words to say, 'God hates treacherous divorce, but he does not hate disciplinary divorce.'[10]

GIVING

In everything I did, I showed you that by this kind of hard work we must help the weak, remembering the words the Lord Jesus himself said: 'It is more blessed to give than to receive.'

Acts 20:35

Foundation

This message is about giving of our finances (or possessions) to God's Kingdom work. The church is included in God's Kingdom, but it is not the same thing. When followers of Jesus look at any subject, they should examine, and interpret, and understand correctly what the Bible says about that subject. We should allow the Bible to speak for itself. We give to the work of the Kingdom of God and that is the storehouse.

What does the Bible say about: money, marriage, sex, singleness, or divorce? I believe Bible teaching is timeless. The Bible teaches us for today's and tomorrow's world. God in His wisdom and love has given us the Holy Bible to guide us by His Holy Spirit.

The Bible teaches that marriage is between a man and a woman. This is true for all time. My African Christian friends will accept the truth of that statement. However, many Christians and sections of the church in the UK, Europe, and America may not accept that Bible statement. It seems people believe what they want to believe to suit their own character, lifestyle, ideas, and performances.

Some people do not like the teaching in the Bible about the Deity of Christ, or hell, so they get rid of that. Scripture trains us in right living. Therefore, as disciples of Jesus, let us come under the word of God. *'All Scripture is God-breathed and is useful for teaching, rebuking, correcting, and training in righteousness, so that the servant of God may be thoroughly equipped for every good work'* (2 Timothy 3:16-17).

The Biggest Blessing

Am I more blessed if I give £200 to God's Kingdom's work rather than someone giving me £200? Honestly, it feels like I am more blessed to receive that gift. However, there are times when, as I have given, it has felt greater than getting. Whether it 'feels' like it or not, giving is greater than receiving. And if I get the 'feeling' that is a bonus. The apostle Paul speaks about the words of Jesus, *'It is more blessed to give than to receive'* (Acts 20:35).

When Christians speak of what wonderful blessings God gave them, it is usually something they have received. But a disciple could say, 'Hallelujah, I received a blessing this week from the Lord. The blessing was that I gave £200 for God's Kingdom. Praise the Lord, I am blessed.'

The Rich Young Man

In this story, Jesus tells this rich young ruler to give away everything to the poor and then follow Him (Mark 10:17-31). The man's face fell. He went away sad because he had great wealth. It is very hard for the rich to enter the Kingdom, says Jesus. This specific man loved money more than Jesus or anything else. My point is this: Jesus did not invite the rich young man to give 10 per cent but 100 per cent. When Jesus asks us to do something radical, He will help us.

Prayer

> *Lord, help me to give my treasure,*
> *To give towards Your Kingdom work.*
> *Lord, may my pocket be converted,*
> *May it belong to You.*
> *Lord, thank You for Your good gifts.*
> *Amen.*

GENEROUS

On the first day of each week, you should each put aside a portion of the money you have earned and save it for this offering.
1 Corinthians 16:2 (NLT)

The Widow's Offering (Mark 12:41-44)

One day Jesus noticed that a widow put into the temple everything she had, although it was meagre or tiny. Jesus tells His disciples on that day people gave large amounts out of their wealth and they still had much; she gave out of her poverty. The widow gave 100 per cent. The widow's mite was everything, 100 per cent. If we give a small or 'mite' away, we should not call it 'the widow's mite' unless it is 100 per cent. This widow was extremely generous. Only do such a thing if Jesus tells you.

Blessing is Blessing (Luke 6:38; Ephesians 3:14-21)

Jesus says give and it will be given to you.

Give, and it will be given to you: good measure, pressed down, shaken together, and running over will be put into your bosom. For with the same measure that you use, it will be measured back to you.

Luke 6:38 (NKJV)

When we give, we will be given, and it is not only or always material. There is pressure, sometimes manipulation in churches (Nigeria, USA), for people to give and they will receive back more money in return. This is wrong. It is evil. The Lord may give back in so many ways, including spiritually. God gives blessings of strength, power, His Spirit and His love and peace.

Give in Keeping with Your Income (1 Corinthians 16:2)

Paul encourages the Christians in Corinth to give in proportion to their income. In their case, it was a weekly matter of giving to the Lord's work. Whatever income we have each week or month from whatever source (salary, pension, etc.), a particular percentage can be given. Sometimes we may give more as the Lord directs and enables. Jesus speaks these words about when giving to the poor or needy:

Be careful not to practise your righteousness in front of others to be seen by them. If you do, you will have no reward from your Father in heaven.

Matthew 6:1

Our heavenly Father rewards (materially and/or spiritually) when He sees what we do in secret. Many wonderful people have given to Soteria Trust for the poor and needy in Nigeria, especially to build the Soteria School in Ibadan, Nigeria. Others give each

172

month to Soteria Trust so we can provide schooling for little children or young people. They do this privately.

One man recently came to the office to give Soteria Trust a large gift. A good man, giving quietly and privately without any fuss. Sometimes, I am overwhelmed by Christians giving to God's Kingdom work.

Should God Repay Us?

There is a popular teaching in churches and on our screens that if you make a (large) gift, God will return it to you and multiply it. God may, and He may well not. If we give to get, we give for the wrong reason and we could be foolish. This is part of the prosperity gospel. It is non-biblical. This extreme prosperity teaching is a means for those preachers to line their own pockets. Many of these teachers or pastors manipulate, control, and dominate their congregations for selfish reasons. God is not mocked.

> *The early church was married to poverty, prisons, and persecutions. Today, the church is married to prosperity, personality, and popularity.*
>
> *Leonard Ravenhill*

Do not be taken in by a testimony from someone who has received a large amount after making a huge donation in church as if that is the way it works, and you do likewise. Know this: multitudes who receive no cash returns remain silent. I would rather listen to God's word through the apostle Paul than Pastor Smick from Nigeria or Pastor Slick from America.

> *Who has ever given to God, that God should repay them?*
>
> *Romans 11:35*

TIME, TALENT, TREASURE

They sold property and possessions to give to anyone who had need.
Acts 2:45

Fellowship of Believers

The early church (Acts 2:41-47) was generous with their treasures. They shared their lives together and had everything in common. They helped each other. They were kind to each other. The believers sold their possessions and shared with those in need. It seems the church leaders did not want to have people in need. The need was met by those who had the means. The Holy Spirit was transforming minds, hearts, and will, so that the poor or needy were taken care of.

They sold property and possessions to give to anyone who had need.

Acts 2:45

Christine, a widow perhaps in her early 40s, approached me at a church meeting in Scotland saying she wanted to help. She gifted her home to Soteria Trust. She was moved by the presentation of our desire to build a school in Nigeria to help educate poor, needy young people. Soteria Trust sold the house and gave all the proceeds towards building the school in Ibadan, Nigeria. Christine, the widow with young sons, donated the only home she owned. She has lived in rented accommodation since. She is not wealthy. The Holy Spirit led her. Christine gave to the work of God's Kingdom, the storehouse, to help build a school in Africa.

Tithing

The New Testament of the Bible has only three references about tithing. None of these are about Christians tithing. Jesus did not say to His disciples in any way at all that they should tithe. In the same way, there is not any instruction or teaching in the New Testament and its writers about tithing. What we do see in the early church is an incredible, generous spirit of giving.

Our treasure is one area that we can give. And there are also our talents and time. I believe we need to give as the Lord prompts in keeping with what we have. It may be 5 per cent, 10 per cent, or more. For the widow in the Bible, it was everything. For the widow in Scotland, it was much more than 10 per cent.

I feel that some Christians cheat God because they only give 10 per cent when they could give more and still be very well off. It is doing what the Holy Spirit tells you. Please do not give from what you do not have. I would like to see disciples of Jesus giving of their God-given resources: treasure, talents, and time.

The Beautiful Life of Nancy

When I was a young boy, a neighbour gave me of her time and talents. Nancy gave me free lessons every week in her home. She did that for about three years. I thank God for her beautiful life and gift to me. I am where I am today because my education was established through a neighbour giving me her time. I proceeded to acquire my engineering qualification in later years. With that I obtained a wonderful job as a design engineer for an excellent company.

Prayer

O Lord, use my talents, treasures, and time
For Your Kingdom and glory.
I offer myself to You, precious Jesus.
Amen.

LEARNING TO WALK SEEN

Then he said to her, 'Daughter, your faith has healed you. Go in peace.'
Luke 8:48

Learning to Walk Seen

One of the main characters in the stage musical *Chicago* is Amos Hart. He calls himself Mr Cellophane as he feels that people can walk right through him without knowing he is there. He feels invisible, unseen, that he does not matter. Have you ever felt like that, invisible or unnoticed or that you do not matter?

The woman who had been bleeding for 12 years must have felt just like that. Invisible. She had been to doctors, spent all she had. But instead of getting better she had got worse. She was tired, worn out, alone, on her own, separate, and invisible. No one wanted anything to do with her. She was dirty, ceremonially unclean. Everything she touched also became unclean.

But she was also desperate. So desperate that she thought, 'If I just touch His clothes, I will be healed.' So desperate that she does

179

not mind who she bumps into or knocks out of the way to get to Jesus. She does what she sets out to do and was healed instantly, but that is not enough for Jesus. Part of her healing and ours is that the INVISIBLE becomes VISIBLE.

Double Blessings

Jesus could have let her leave physically healed and that would have been the end. That was not enough for Jesus. His heart's desire is for her to be *fully* healed, *fully* restored. Would she have been content to be only physically healed? Jesus wanted to give her a double blessing. He wanted her physically and emotionally healed. All her life she had been publicly put down but now Jesus was going to publicly affirm her.

She was seen by Jesus, but now Jesus wanted her to be seen by the disciples and by the crowd. Jesus provides an opportunity for her to receive more, by saying:

> *'Someone touched me; I know that power has gone out from me.'*
> *Then the woman, seeing that she could not go unnoticed, came*
> *trembling and fell at his feet.*
>
> Luke 8:46-47

Jesus wanted her to be noticed by Him and others and invited her to tell her story publicly. In the presence of all the people, she told why she had touched Him and how she had been instantly healed. She came to Jesus and came in front of the crowd. For the first time in over 12 years, she was seen not unseen. Visible not invisible. Clean, no longer unclean. Outcast to daughter. Unknown to known. Worthless to precious. Unloved to loved.

Jesus wanted the woman to be physically and emotionally healed, enjoying that personal relationship with Him. Face to face. The woman received a double healing. A miracle within a miracle. Not only healed physically but emotionally. Jesus restored her to the world. Jesus restored the world to her. How wonderful is that?

GOD SEES AND LOVES

Indeed, the very hairs of your head are all numbered. Don't be afraid; you are worth more than many sparrows.

Luke 12:7

The Woman

She got more than she wanted. She is not only healed physically but healed emotionally. She would have been restored back into the community. She would have known how much she was seen by Jesus and loved by Jesus. Jesus's disciples and the crowd now had an opportunity to learn important lessons for themselves from the woman's healing.

The Disciples

As usual for the disciples, this was a steep learning curve for them. A miraculous healing. Stretched and challenged on how to demonstrate love. Loving those who the world discards and does not love. Learning how to restore people back to their rightful place in the world. Restoring the outcast. Learning what it means to be a true follower of Jesus. Putting godly love into practice.

The Crowd

They were being challenged firstly by the miracle itself and secondly by the restoration of the woman. Challenged on their attitudes towards the woman and to this Messiah, Jesus.

Summing Up

One of the Old Testament names for God is El Roi – the God who sees me. It is used only once in the Bible in Genesis 16:13 by Hagar, an Egyptian slave, the mother of Abraham's eldest son, Ishmael, when she encountered God in the desert and called Him El Roi, *'The God who sees me.'* Hagar's God is the One who not only numbers the hairs on our heads, but also knows our circumstances: past, present, and future. The God who sees me.

One of the most powerful images of being seen is in Genesis 2:25, *'And they were both naked, the man and his wife, and were not ashamed'* (NKJV). Adam and Eve were seen by God – they were visible, nothing hidden, walking with God.

For our well-being in mind and spirit, we need to know that we are children of the light and are seen by God and by others. We have nothing to fear by being seen; it is the best way that we can continue our relationship with Him and is the best way to walk.

Application

What might it take for us to be able to walk seen and for us to see others? Are we happy and content with just one blessing?

Learning to Walk Upright

And a woman was there who had been crippled by a spirit for eighteen years. She was bent over and could not straighten up at all.

Luke 13:11

Learning to Walk Upright

L earning to walk seen leads to learning to walk upright. In the previous section, 'Learning to Walk Seen', the healing is initiated by the desperation of the woman.

In the case of the woman crippled by a spirit for eighteen years, she was bent over and could not straighten up at all, it was Jesus who initiated it, by calling her forward.

Jesus saw her and healed her. Enabling her to walk upright. Jesus wants us to be able to walk upright too. No longer bent over but looking up. No longer ashamed but unashamed. No longer insecure and self-conscious but secure in who we are in Him.

When Everton was Six

When I was a small boy, about six years old, I remember a relative would come and visit on Sundays and, when she was leaving, my brother and I would line up at the door to say good-bye and she would kiss us. Every time she came, she would say the same thing to me, 'I have not come to see you, I have come to see your younger brother. You are the ugly one, he is the pretty one.' I think I tried to laugh it off. Neither she nor I realised the effect, the damage, these words spoken over me would do. I walked bent down for so many years. It has taken a long time, with God's love, the love of my wife, and others, to break the power of those words. I now know that I am not ugly, but I am beautiful.

When Everton was a Vicar

When I was speaking at a church meeting held in a hall, which was also a dance studio (it had large mirrors on the walls), I was talking about how God sees us. As I was speaking, I felt God ask me to get the people that were there to stand, and ask them to look in the mirror and tell me what they saw.

The first thing I noticed was that the women found the task incredibly hard to do; the men were marginally better, but not much. As people were looking into the mirrors, I asked them to tell me what they saw. These were some of the answers: too fat, ugly, big ears or not slim enough. 'How self-condemning, seeing ourselves as the world sees us,' I said. All words which are not from a loving heavenly Father but from a liar, a thief, an enemy, who seeks to steal, kill, and destroy.

Now listen to what God says about you, how God sees you.

You are loved – You are the apple of His eye – You are a child of God – You are beautiful – You are unique – You are special – You are precious – You are called to freedom – You are no longer condemned – You are alive in Him – You are a new person – You are mine – He has made you – He thinks about you and cares for you – You are blessed.

Wonderful truths which enable us to stand upright, no longer bent over.

FREE

But you, LORD, are a shield around me, my glory, the One who lifts my head high.

Psalm 3:3

Nelson Mandela

Mandela spent 18 of his 27 years of imprisonment on Robben Island. He was known as 'prisoner 46664' – the 466th prisoner to arrive in 1964 (466/64). Life on Robben Island was very harsh, especially for political prisoners. He was classified as the lowest grade of inmate, class D, which meant he received the least privileges, the hardest punishments, and the worst living conditions.

He was allowed one letter and one visit every six months. His eight-foot by seven-foot cell had no plumbing. There was a bucket for a toilet. His bed was a straw mat. He had no pyjamas to keep him warm as he slept on the cold damp floor, a privilege that was provided only to white prisoners. His early days were spent breaking rocks with a hammer before being reassigned to digging in a blindingly bright lime quarry. This task permanently damaged Nelson's eyesight, since he was forbidden to wear sunglasses.

Can you imagine on 11th February 1990? The prison doors are opened, and Nelson Mandela is invited to leave, as he is free. But instead of leaving, he chooses to stay where he is, in prison. That is what we so often do. Jesus has opened the prison door, set us free. By His death on the cross, He has won our freedom.

The Lord Lifts Up My Head

Jesus invites us to live a life of fullness and freedom. He invites us to leave the prison. But we have so many objections like:

- I do not know what freedom looks like
- I am familiar with my prison cell
- It has become home to me
- There is a sense of familiarity and security here
- I think I will stay where I am

That does not make sense and of course we know that Nelson Mandela walked out of the prison and achieved many great things afterwards. The woman who was crippled, bent over, had been set free from her prison. Set free from her infirmities, the first thing she did was to praise God. She walked out of her prison, to freedom.

Application

What might it take for us to walk upright?

The prison doors are open, and Jesus beckons us out.
Lazarus, come out. [Insert your name], come out!

Jesus sees us and wants us to straighten up, He is the lifter of our head. As we encounter Him, He enables us to straighten up. He gives us a sense of worth, acceptance, love, forgiveness, peace, hope, and life in all its fullness. Learn to walk upright.

CHARLES SPURGEON

Am I now trying to win the approval of human beings, or of God? Or am I trying to please people? If I were still trying to please people, I would not be a servant of Christ.

Galatians 1:10

Charles Haddon Spurgeon (1834–1892)
Preacher and Pastor

Spurgeon is known as the Prince of Preachers. Thousands listened to him and read his words. As many as 25,000 copies of his sermons were produced on a weekly basis and could be purchased for a penny. In Scotland, news stands on railway station platforms carried his sermons.

The Metropolitan Tabernacle was built during his ministry to accommodate great crowds and he built up a congregation of almost 5,500. Spurgeon's famous and well-loved voice has been described as, 'A melody with an immense scale of tones.' And yet, some 130 years after his death, what is said of Abel is most certainly true of Spurgeon: *'Even though he is dead, he still speaks through his faith'* (Hebrews 11:4, CSB). His sermons and books have remained in print and continue to inform and influence generations of preachers, Christians, and non-Christians alike.

Diluted Christianity and Liberal Views

Spurgeon was more than a great preacher; he was prophetic in words, nature, and action like that of John the Baptist. Spurgeon's convictions while very young were deepened with time. This helps to explain his strong resistance to a diluted Christianity which he saw in the Baptist Union's liberal views of biblical inspiration and the nature and work of the atonement or cross of Jesus. Spurgeon decided to speak and write against the church's downgrading of biblical truths. His withdrawal from the Baptist Union sparked the greatest controversy of his life. The 'Downgrade Controversy'. He was opposed by many of his closest friends and students, including alumni from his pastors' college.

> *I cannot tell you by letter what I have endured in the desertion of my own men.*
>
> *Spurgeon's letter to a friend,*
> *21st February 1888*

James, Spurgeon's own brother, turned against him. The distress affected his health, and it has been suggested that the controversy killed Spurgeon at 57 years of age. However, the masses loved Spurgeon; 60,000 people paid their respects during the three days Spurgeon's body lay in state at the Metropolitan Tabernacle. An estimated 100,000 people lined the streets as his hearse made its way to the cemetery. The flags were at half-mast and the shops and pubs were closed.

Looking Unto Jesus

A dear friend gave me a copy of Spurgeon's daily devotional. It has proved to be of help and an encouragement. From Spurgeon's *Morning and Evening* little devotional book (June 28) commenting on 'Looking unto Jesus' from Hebrews 12:2, he writes:

> *We shall never find happiness by looking at our prayers, our doings, or our feelings; it is what **Jesus is,** not what **we are**, that gives rest to the Soul.* [11]

Spurgeon Quotes

> ***You and I*** *cannot be useful if we want to be sweet as honey in the mouths of men. God will never bless us if we wish to please men, that they think well of us. Are you willing to tell them what will break your own heart in the telling and break theirs in the hearing? If not, you are not fit to serve the Lord. You must be willing to go and speak for God, though you will be rejected.*

> ***A time will*** *come when instead of shepherds feeding the sheep, the church will have clowns entertaining the goats.*

> ***I believe that*** *one reason why the church of God at this present moment has so little influence over the world is because the world has so much influence over the church.*

> ***Satan always hates*** *Christian fellowship; it is his policy to keep Christians apart. Anything which can divide saints from one another he delights in. Since union is strength, he does his best to promote separation.*

DWIGHT MOODY

Since we live by the Spirit, let us keep in step with the Spirit.

Galatians 5:25

Dwight Lyman Moody (1837–1899) Evangelist

Dwight Lyman Moody was born in Northfield, Massachusetts, the sixth of nine children. Moody's mother was widowed when he was four years old. He devoted his life to serving God after his Sunday school teacher, Edward Kimball, led him to the Lord. Moody writes:

> *One day as I recollected, my Sunday school teacher came around behind the counter of the shop where I was at work, and put his hand on my shoulder, and talked to me about Christ and my soul. I had not felt that I had a soul until then. I said to myself, 'This is a very strange thing. Here is a man who never saw me till lately, and he is weeping over my sins, and I never shed a tear about them.' But I understood about it now and know what it is to have a passion for men's souls and weep over their sins.*

I do not remember what he said, but I can feel the power of that man's hand on my shoulder tonight. It was not long after that I was brought into the Kingdom of God. [12]

Passion for People's Souls

In 1871, while Moody was finishing a sermon, Chicago's fire alarm bells began to ring. It is today known as the Great Fire of Chicago. The fire laid waste a third of the city, killed nearly two hundred people, and left over 17,000 homeless. In response, Moody was crying all the time God would fill him with His Spirit, when he had such an experience of His love that he had to ask Him to stay His hand.

From that time on, Moody asked God to help him win at least one soul a day; he never missed. Moody is said to have once witnessed to a woman but her husband was annoyed saying, 'Why didn't you tell him to mind his own business?' 'If you had seen the look on his face and the way he talked, you would have known it was his business,' she replied.

Moody spoke to more people about Christ than any other man in history up to his time. What was needed was neither the recognition nor ordination of man; what really counted was the touch and the hand of God on ordinary people who were wholly consecrated to Him.

Moody was born again of the Holy Spirit at conversion. Later he was baptised with the Holy Spirit and fire. Moody learned to live by the Holy Spirit daily and he learned to keep in step with the Holy Spirit.

Moody Quotes

I fought against it for months, but the best thing I ever did was when I surrendered my will and let the will of God be done in me.

I have never met a man who has given me as much trouble as myself.

I look upon this world as a wrecked vessel, God has given me a lifeboat and said, 'Moody, save all you can.'

Set yourself on fire and people will come and watch you burn.

ARTHUR KATZ

I baptise you with water for repentance. But after me comes one who is more powerful than I, whose sandals I am not worthy to carry. He will baptise you with the Holy Spirit and fire.

Matthew 3:11

Arthur Katz (1929–2007) Preacher and Evangelist

Katz was a Jewish college lecturer in America and Europe. Arthur Katz, a bitter Marxist-existentialist philosopher, was converted in Israel on a journey to find his roots while reading the story of Jesus speaking to the woman taken in adultery.

When I was studying engineering in London, I attended an evening evangelistic outreach lecture arranged by the Christian Union with a guest speaker, Arthur Katz (then 47 years old). Katz was the most powerful and compelling speaker I have ever heard. Some of my friends from class attended the meeting, including Ali my Muslim friend. At the end of the meeting students could ask their personal questions to Arthur Katz.

The Presence of God. Revival

Ali was deeply challenged by Katz's talk and was deeply, visibly, and emotionally moved. I could see it in his face and hear it in his voice. Ali was afraid to ask Katz his question and asked me if I could ask on his behalf. Ali and I queued patiently, and I finally stepped forward (with Ali close by) to ask the question. Upon hearing the question, Katz looked at Ali and said to him, 'Why did you not ask your own question?' Ali was further challenged as if he was speaking to a prophet or someone who could tell you what you had for breakfast.

From my own experience of having met Arthur Katz, I can testify that what is written of him in *The Revival Study Bible* is true:

> *Katz's profound preaching in colleges, universities, and seminaries were marked by powerful manifestations of the presence of God in wholly secular environments.*[13]

Katz quotes

> **God does not** *want the faith of men to be established on eloquence, but on the basis of the power of God.*

> **There is a** *price to pay for integrity; for guarding your spirit and heart. If you are not willing to pay it, you will be swept away with the age.*

> **Any preaching that** *is not anointed is not preaching but mere oratory.*

> **The anointing is** *my life. If I am not in the anointing of God, woe unto me, and those who are hearing me.*

George Verwer

Therefore confess your sins to each other and pray for each other so that you may be healed. The prayer of a righteous person is powerful and effective.

James 5:16

George Verwer, DD (1938–Present)
Missionary and Evangelist

George Verwer is a passionate advocate of radical discipleship as the only legitimate option for people who believe in Jesus. George was converted at a Billy Graham crusade in Madison Square Garden in New York City at the age of 16. Before that, a praying woman was interceding for both George's conversion and him becoming a missionary. God answered.

Within a year, Verwer saw more than 120 of his classmates commit themselves to Christ. Soon, George founded Operation Mobilisation (OM), which each year sends thousands of people – and places countless Bibles, books, and tracts throughout the world – on a mission of evangelism, discipleship training, leadership training, and church planting in some 80 countries.

Today OM has many hundreds of staff, workers, or volunteers in the world. George and his wife Drena live in the UK and continue to train leaders, pastors in evangelism and discipleship under Operation Mobilisation Special Projects. George, an evangelist and a penetrating preacher, is a man of compassion and passion for a lost world and Jesus's church.

The Revolution of Love

When I was 20 years old, I read George Verwer's book *The Revolution of Love.* The message within those pages still assists me today. George was the guest speaker at a men's church breakfast meeting. We spoke at the gathering and I felt a connection. He kindly gave me many of his books that day which I distributed to young people at our mission school in Nigeria.

George emailed me recently. His words were most encouraging. I felt it was the word of the Lord. The printed message is displayed on my kitchen cupboard. It reminds me of God's love and word for me from a man called George.

Confessions of A Toxic Perfectionist

George Verwer writes in his excellent book, *Confessions of A Toxic Perfectionist and God's Antidote,* about some of the most important things he has learned:

I have had an extra special interest in couples who met on OM, but those marriages broke. Well over a thousand couples have met on OM, especially on our four different ships. OM actually pioneered in accepting divorced people coming into global missions. We now have a long history of outstanding divorced people being used of God. I believe it is wrong teaching and toxic perfectionism that led to the persecution and mistreatment of divorced people for a couple of thousand years.[14]

George Verwer Quotes

We who have Christ's eternal life need to throw away our own lives.

If only we could see the value of one soul like God does.

The truth is that most mission work is carried out where the church already exists. Only small percentages are working where the church is non-existent.

JEAN DARNALL

When Jesus saw Nathanael approaching, he said of him, 'Here truly is an Israelite in whom there is no deceit.' 'How do you know me?' Nathanael asked. Jesus answered, 'I saw you while you were still under the fig-tree before Philip called you.'

John 1:47-48

If the Holy Spirit were withdrawn from the church today, 95 per cent of what we do would go on and no one would know the difference.
A. W. Tozer (1897–1963)

Jean Darnall (1923–2019) Pastor and Evangelist

Jean Darnall, from Toledo, Ohio, USA, was a long-time Foursquare pastor, missionary, evangelist, and author with a strong prophetic gifting. Her family did not attend church when she was growing up. However, after Jean was diagnosed with a serious kidney infection at the age of 16, her mother sought out a church after seeing their advertisement which included the words, 'Jesus heals.' Jean experienced healing after the female evangelist prayed for her. So did her father, whose lungs had been damaged by chlorine gas during World War I.

This experience, together with a prophecy and word given to Jean by evangelist Kathryn Kuhlman, launched her on a path to a lifetime of ministry over seven decades in the USA, Australia, Panama, Canada, and the UK where she lived for 25 years. Jean and her husband Elmer were strong believers in the baptism and power of the Holy Spirit. They played a key role in charismatic renewal in the UK. Jean preached in many Anglican churches and was greatly respected.

Prophecy

Prophecy is to forthtell and/or foretell the word of the Lord. Prophecy is needed today more than ever. Nearly 30 years ago, I attended an annual evangelists' conference in Swanwick, England. During one meeting we got into small groups to pray together. Our group had just finished, but others were still praying. A lady approached me and quietly said, 'I believe I have a word for you from the Lord. Can I tell you it?' It was Jean Darnall and I was happy. The essence of what she said was this:

> I see you with a microphone in one hand and a notebook in the other. From your notebook you are preaching other people's words and sermons. Put the notebook away. You are unique and original. Again, I see you on a platform with your Bible in one hand and a microphone in the other. You are speaking powerfully God's word from the Bible to thousands. You are unique and original. Be so.

Somehow, by the gift of the Holy Spirit given to her, Jean Darnall knew something of my past, what I was like, and predicted something about my future. Concerning the future, it came true. It was true that I had been using other preachers' sermons. The emphasis on being unique and original was helpful and challenging for my formation. The part about speaking to large crowds with my Bible and a microphone was to be fulfilled sooner than I knew. Three months later my first international evangelistic mission started.

Thank God for the sweet and sensitive spirit that dwelt within Jean Darnall. Thank the Father, Son, and Holy Spirit that lived within her life for God's glory. I was and I am still personally grateful to Jean who walked across the room to speak the word of the Lord. Evan Roberts said that for revival to come, we need to obey the leading of the Holy Spirit, promptly.

GEORGE MULLER

In the same way, count yourselves dead to sin but alive to God in Christ Jesus.

Romans 6:11

George Muller (1805–1895) Philanthropist and Evangelist

George Muller was an intercessor, missionary to children, philanthropist, and evangelist. He read through the Bible over two hundred times, half of that on his knees. God put it into his heart to build five orphanages, with only two shillings (10p) in his pockets without making his needs known to anyone but God alone. Muller testified:

> *In the greatest difficulties, in the heaviest trials, in the deepest poverty and necessities, He has never failed me.*

George Muller supported 21,000 children over the 54 years he was in charge, accommodating up to 2,000 orphans at a time. He gave gifts of about 300,000 Bibles in many different languages, in addition to 1.5 million New Testaments of the Bible. He sent out or supported 163 missionaries and distributed over 111 million tracts in a period of 63 years, all by faith alone.

God Orders Our Stops

At the age of 70, George Muller began to make great evangelistic tours. He travelled 200,000 miles, going around the world and preaching the Good News in many lands and in several different languages, speaking to up to 4,500 in a single gathering. Three times he preached throughout the length and breadth of the United States.

During 17 years of gospel work, he addressed three million people and all his expenses were sent in answer to the prayer of faith. There was a day when George Muller died (to self) and therefore did not live any longer for himself and for the approval of others. But Muller lived for God's approval alone. We have a long way to go. George Muller said:

> *There was a day when I died; died to self, my opinions, preferences, tastes and will; died to the world, its approval or censure; died to the approval or blame even of my brethren or friends; and since then, I have studied only to show myself approved unto God.*

George Muller Quotes

> *The Christian should never worry about tomorrow or give sparingly because of possible future need. Only the present moment is ours to serve the Lord, and tomorrow may never come . . . Life is worth as much as it is spent for the Lord's service.*

> *Our heavenly Father never takes anything from His children unless He means to give them something better.*

> *God not only orders our steps, but He also orders our stops.*

Endnotes

[1] Derek Prince, *Prophetic Guide to the End Times*
(Chosen Books, 2008), pp. 53-54.

[2] Anthony Chamberlain, *The Promise of the Father*
(Zaccmedia, 2017), p. 41.

[3] R.T. Kendall, *Holy Fire* (Destiny Image, 2014), p. 47.

[4] Watchman Nee, *The Normal Christian Life*
(Kingsway, 1961), p. 31.

[5] George Verwer, *The Revolution of Love,*
(GS Books, 1989), pp. 19-20.

[6] Anthony Chamberlain, *The Promise of the Father,* p. 67.

[7] Anthony Chamberlain, *The Promise of the Father,* p. 49.

[8] Anthony Chamberlain, *The Promise of the Father,* p. 157.

[9] Barbara Roberts, *Not Under Bondage; Biblical Divorce for Abuse,
Adultery and Desertion,* (Maschil Press, 2008), pp. 127, 129.

[10] Barbara Roberts, *Not Under Bondage,* p. 113.

[11] C.H. Spurgeon, *Morning and Evening*
(Christian Focus, 1994), p. 378.

[12] *The Revival Study Bible NKJV* (Genesis Books, 2010), p. 1197.

[13] *The Revival Study Bible NKJV,* p. xv.

[14] George Verwer DD, *Confessions of A Toxic Perfectionist and God's
Antidote* (Good Shepherd Books, 2020), pp. 46-47.

SPONSORSHIP CHANGES LIVES

Soteria Trust is a registered charity based in Emsworth, Hampshire, with Revd Andy Economides the founding director. Soteria Trust helps vulnerable young people (aged 16 plus) including those who have no parents, those who are extremely poor, or women who could be sexually exploited. Young people are awarded scholarships to study at the Soteria Business School in Ibadan, Nigeria, West Africa. Soteria Trust also provides sponsorship for Soteria School staff.

Children (aged 4–18 years) who are poor or needy are also awarded sponsorships to attend Prospect School in Ibadan – a combined primary and secondary school which Revd Andy Economides helped to build by raising funds to purchase the land.

You can make a difference by sponsoring a young person, child, or staff worker for £19 per month. You can sponsor more than one if you wish. Please ask for a pack for your kind consideration. Email us on admin@ soteriatrust.org.uk, telephone on 01243 377315 or return the slip below.

Please send me a sponsorship pack for

❑ Child ❑ Young Person ❑ Soteria School Staff

❑ I don't mind who I sponsor (apply to greatest need)

My name (BLOCK CAPITALS):

....

My address: ....

....

.... Post code: ....

My phone no: ....

My email: ....

SPONSORSHIP

Please return this slip to:
Soteria Trust, 39 North Street, Emsworth, Hampshire, PO10 7DA, UK

Sponsorship Changes Lives

My name is Ola★: I was given a scholarship at SBS by Revd Andy to study Administration, Business & Computing and later awarded a scholarship to study ATS – Accounting Technician Scheme. I was able to proceed to polytechnic for HND with my AAT certificate and undergo the National Youth Service Corps.
I worked a few years since 2014 with my International Diploma certificate from Chichester College and later was able to set up my own Creative Digital Agency here in Ibadan. We design websites. The course at Soteria Business School has been so helpful and I can say I am a better person today. God bless Revd Andy and my sponsor.

My name is Francis★: I came to the Soteria Business School and was awarded a scholarship with feeding and accommodation. I was also fed with the word of God all through my stay. After my two-year course in Administration, Business and IT at SBS I was able to get a job with the diploma given to me by the school to work as
an IT Administrator. With this job, I was able to feed myself and help my family. I have an admission to study nursing in a nursing college in Ogun State Nigeria. I am grateful to God and Soteria Trust for the great privilege as my ambition is finally coming to pass.

★ Names have been changed.

**To sponsor please return the slip on the previous page
or call the Soteria Office**

SOTERIA BUSINESS SCHOOL
Ibadan, Nigeria, West Africa

Soteria Business School (SBS) is an Innovation Enterprise Institution approved by the Ministry of Education of Nigeria. SBS is affiliated to Chichester College in the United Kingdom. SBS provides training and awards national diplomas. The professional courses include:

- NID Business Informatics
- NID Software Engineering
- NID Hardware Engineering
- Accounting Technician Scheme (ATS)
- Data Processing
- Software and Hardware Engineering
- Website Design
- Microsoft Applications and Desktop Publishing

Soteria Business School provides excellent teaching and hostel facilities with affordable fees. The school has a well-equipped library and computer rooms. SBS has a solar system which supplies regular and better electricity.

The Vision of Soteria Business School

- Education for Jobs
- Values: Excellence, Honesty, Compassion and Determination
- Teaching Christ in Word and Action

For more information:

You are welcome to visit. Register for full-time or part-time courses from 3 months to 2 years. The Soteria Business School has courses Monday to Friday and Saturday for specific professional studies. Come and see for yourself.

Soteria Business School, Beside DB Petrol Station, Bola-Ige Bus Stop, Liberty Road, Oke-Ado, Ibadan, Nigeria.

Tel: +234 (0)703 0049999, +234 (0)802 7685159

Email: soteriabusinessschool@gmail.com

Website: www.soteriaschool.com

RESOURCES AVAILABLE

TRUE

If you are a Christian this book will refresh your soul by showing you Jesus Christ again. If you have never seen Jesus Christ clearly, in these pages you will see him standing before you. And when our tired, unseeing eyes are opened to glimpse him, he is indeed the most beautiful sight for sore eyes.

From the foreword by J.John.

Sale price: £5 Normally: £6.99

TRUE RELATIONSHIPS

Blessing others; forgiving others; loving others; love, sex and marriage; the greatest friendship – mentoring; the impacting friendships of leaders; relationships to avoid; recovering from spiritual abuse; divorce and remarriage; trust; singleness; friendship with Christ.

Sale price: £5 Normally: £8.99

**These books are available from the Soteria Office
and can also be ordered by completing the slip on page 221**

RESOURCES AVAILABLE

REFRESHED & RENEWED

Provides a weekly word for daily living for the whole year with 53 short chapters. Refreshed and Renewed looks at the life of Jesus Christ and His transforming power today by taking us through the gospel of John for 21 weeks. This is Andy Economides's first weekly word for daily living (with hardback).

Sale price: £10 Normally: £12

HE HATES OR GOD HATES
– Malachi 2:16

Revd Andy Economides book examines who is doing the hating in Malachi 2:16, to discover whether it is the man or God. This book carefully looks at the Bible's teaching about divorce, remarriage and singleness. A pastoral book bringing healing and truth..

Sale price: £7 Normally: £9

**These books are available from the Soteria Office
and can also be ordered by completing the slip on page 221**

RESOURCES AVAILABLE

RESTORED & REVIVED
- HARDBACK WITH RIBBON

Here are 52 meditations. This is book is typically Andy: wise, practical and distilled from many decades of a faithful walk with Jesus. He has sown seeds here for you to water and nurture into flourishing plants. A long time ago I listened to what he said, and I am very grateful that I did. May you have the same experience!

From the foreword by J.John.

Sale price: £12 Normally: £15

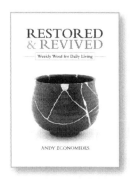

RESTORED & REVIVED
- SOFTBACK

Here are 52 meditations. This is book is typically Andy: wise, practical and distilled from many decades of a faithful walk with Jesus. He has sown seeds here for you to water and nurture into flourishing plants. A long time ago I listened to what he said, and I am very grateful that I did. May you have the same experience!

From the foreword by J.John.

Sale price: £10 Normally: £12

**These books are available from the Soteria Office
and can also be ordered by completing the slip opposite**

MY RESPONSE SLIP

My information request

❏ I would like to receive Soteria News regularly.

My regular giving

❏ Send me information on how I can give regularly to Soteria Trust.

My one-off gift

❏ I enclose a gift of £ .... for Soteria Trust.

All cheques should be made payable to SOTERIA TRUST and sent with slip.

My order	Cost	P&P	Quantity	Total
True	£5	free		
True Relationships	£5	free		
Refreshed & Renewed	£10	free		
He Hates or God Hates	£7	free		
Restored & Revived (hardback)	£12	free		
Restored & Revived (softback)	£10	free		
			TOTAL	

My name (BLOCK CAPITALS):

....

My address: ....

....

.... Post code: ....

My phone no: ....

My email: ....

Please return this slip to:
Soteria Trust, 39 North Street, Emsworth, Hampshire, PO10 7DA, UK